Praise for *Discovering the Leader in You*

"An excellent guide for both new and seasoned leaders on the unique and complex challenges of leadership in the 21st century. This well-written, concise book will take you through the steps needed to make conscious, deliberate leadership choices in our 24/7 world of constant access and rapid change—choices that will help you better shape and control the influence you want to have."

—**Molly Corbett Broad,** president, American Council on Education

"When managers or executives drift into leadership positions, simply as a step in their careers, they can find themselves tossed about by change and complexity. The authors of *Discovering the Leader in You* plot the coordinates of values and visions against which leaders can set their compass and navigate unknown seas. I highly recommend this book for emerging and established leaders."

—**Robert W. Bryan,** CFO and SVP, Roll International Corporation

"Leaders are made, not born. Effective leadership requires deep passion, an unwavering commitment to serving others, a bold vision of future possibilities, and a conscious commitment to lifelong learning. The authors, all associated with the world-renowned Center for Creative Leadership, have written a book that will help leaders in all sectors of society enhance their leadership skills and, in turn, improve the human condition."

—**Shirley Chater,** Ph.D., R.N., former commissioner, U.S. Social Security Administration; president emerita, Texas Woman's University

"Being a leader can be one of the most gratifying roles in life. *Discovering the Leader in You* spells out an effective process that leaders or aspiring leaders can go through to unleash their ability to effect change in the world. This is a compelling book that I recommend highly."

—**Vice Admiral Cutler Dawson (USN Retired),** president and CEO, Navy Federal Credit Union

"King, Altman, and Lee have written an important book that will reward those who are willing to learn, improve, and think expansively about personal passion and growth."

—**Ben Feder,** CEO, Take Two Interactive Software

"Discover who you are as a leader with the world's top experts on the subject!"

—**Marshall Goldsmith,** world-renowned executive coach; author of the *New York Times* best sellers *MOJO* and *What Got You Here Won't Get You There*

"Where does leadership fit in your life? Readers can count on this book to help them answer this question confidently. The authors weave compelling stories of leadership in action with their own extensive coaching experiences to make this book an engaging, active force for creating the leadership our world calls for and deserves."

—**General John W. Handy (USAF retired),** president, JHandy Consulting

"Strong leadership is one key to a healthy and vibrant organization. Building a cadre of leaders who can navigate the challenges ahead is the work of our educational institutions. *Discovering the Leader in You* helps by providing a practical road map for emerging leaders to examine who they are as leaders and which opportunities present the best fit with their style, strengths, and experiences."

—**Nathan O. Hatch,** president, Wake Forest University

"Most leadership books give you answers, but too few ask pointed questions so that you can reflect on and come up with your own answers. *Discovering the Leader in You* does exactly that—and hence it is an important book. Read it."

—**Prasad Kaipa,** Ph.D., CEO coach and advisor, Kaipa Group

"Through their hands-on work unlocking the leadership skills of numerous CCL classes, these authors have distilled the leadership discovery process and key behaviors into an engaging and easy-to-read book. Everyone can learn to build on his or her unique strengths and become a more inspiring leader."

—**Harlan Kent,** CEO, Yankee Candle Company

"All great leaders strive for excellence by committing and periodically recommitting to self-improvement. In *Discovering the Leader in You*, the authors help leaders hone their awareness of self and environment in this must-read guide on the journey to betterment."

—**Risa Lavizzo-Mourey,** M.D., MBA, president, Robert Wood Johnson Foundation

"The most effective leaders know who they are, why they want to lead, what they want to accomplish, how they can lead authentically, and how their experience teaches valuable lessons. The authors of *Discovering the Leader in You* help emerging and experienced leaders gain more clarity about these very issues so that they lead with more purpose and navigate the challenges and rewards of leadership."

—**Kim Martin,** president/general manager, WE tv and Wedding Central

"In *Discovering the Leader in You*, CCL continues a rich tradition of drawing insight from the study of leadership while also presenting a tangible call to action for the practicing leader. What is distinct in this work is how CCL speaks to both the 'formal' leader—someone with a title or job description that embodies leadership—and the 'informal' leader—the person who steps up and takes on a community service project or a role on a school board. The authors ask us to reflect on the question, 'Why do I want to lead?' In a world that appears more and more self-centered, the call for leadership has never been more important. This book inspires us to be intentional in the impact we want to have at home, at work, and in our communities and to step up and lead toward this purpose."

—**Steve Merrill,** VP of Human Resources, OGE Energy Corp.

"An effective leader has to have keen self-awareness, which can only be obtained through a systematic process of self-discovery and evaluation. This book will take you through a proven discovery process that will help hone your leadership skills. I highly recommend it."

—**Donna Noce,** president, White House Black Market

"Leaders are increasingly called upon to lead in a world that is rapidly changing, complex, and uncertain. The authors of *Discovering the Leader in You* have done a marvelous job in calling out the key dimensions of effective leadership for these times of challenge and opportunity. I heartily recommend this book."

—**Nenad Pacek,** president and founder, Global Success Advisors Ltd., Oberwaltersdorf, Austria

"This book has plenty of practical advice about how to be an effective leader. It will make a notable contribution to each leader's reflective journey. The ideas will spark renewed energy for readers with years of leadership experience and provide sound advice to individuals who are new to leadership."

—**Kristen M. Swanson,** Ph.D., R.N., F.A.A.N., dean and Alumni Distinguished Professor, School of Nursing, University of North Carolina, Chapel Hill

"*Discovering the Leader in You* isn't about finding what's inside you or recovering what you've lost. It's about recognizing your situation, embracing its challenges, and making the necessary changes to overcome the challenges you face. This book helps leaders at all levels frame leadership discovery as a choice—a decision to make a difference to improve the lives of other people. Leadership is essential no matter the situation."

—**General James D. Thurman,** commanding general, U.S. Army Forces Command

"Leaders can make or break an organization. With *Discovering the Leader in You*, the authors supply us with a systematic approach to excelling as a leader. The principles defined in this book can help you become the effective, impactful leader you want to be!"

—**Eric Wiseman,** chairman, president, and CEO, VF Corporation

DISCOVERING THE LEADER IN YOU

How to Realize Your Leadership Potential

New and Revised

SARA N. KING

DAVID G. ALTMAN

ROBERT J. LEE

Center for
Creative
Leadership
NORTH AMERICA EUROPE ASIA
www.ccl.org

 JOSSEY-BASS
A Wiley Imprint
www.josseybass.com

Published by Jossey-Bass
A Wiley Imprint
989 Market Street, San Francisco, CA 94103-1741—www.josseybass.com

Readers should be aware that Internet Web sites offered as citations and/or sources for further information may have changed or disappeared between the time this was written and when it is read.

Limit of Liability/Disclaimer of Warranty: While the publisher and author have used their best efforts in preparing this book, they make no representations or warranties with respect to the accuracy or completeness of the contents of this book and specifically disclaim any implied warranties of merchantability or fitness for a particular purpose. No warranty may be created or extended by sales representatives or written sales materials. The advice and strategies contained herein may not be suitable for your situation. You should consult with a professional where appropriate. Neither the publisher nor author shall be liable for any loss of profit or any other commercial damages, including but not limited to special, incidental, consequential, or other damages.

Jossey-Bass books and products are available through most bookstores. To contact Jossey-Bass directly call our Customer Care Department within the U.S. at 800-956-7739, outside the U.S. at 317-572-3986, or fax 317-572-4002.

Jossey-Bass also publishes its books in a variety of electronic formats. Some content that appears in print may not be available in electronic books.

Library of Congress Cataloging-in-Publication Data

King, Sara N.
  Discovering the leader in you : how to realize your leadership potential / Sara N. King, David G. Altman, Robert J. Lee.—New and rev. ed.
    p. cm. —(A joint publication of the Jossey-Bass Business & management series and the Center for Creative Leadership)
  Earlier ed. entered under: Robert J. Lee.
  Includes bibliographical references and index.
  ISBN 978-0-470-49888-0 (cloth); ISBN 978-0-470-90225-6 (ebk);
  ISBN 978-0-470-90228-0 (ebk); ISBN 978-0-470-90230-2 (ebk)
 1. Leadership. I. Altman, David G. II. Lee, Robert J., 1939- III. Lee, Robert J., 1939- Discovering the leader in you. IV. Title.
  HD57.7.L439 2011
  658.4′092—dc22

                                                                    2010032373

Printed in the United States of America
Revised Edition
HB Printing   10 9 8 7 6 5 4 3 2 1

A Joint Publication of

The Jossey-Bass

Business & Management Series

and

The Center for Creative Leadership

CONTENTS

PREFACE

O ver many years, we have had the privilege of working with a large number of senior leaders and managers from different organizations all over the world. While many of them have impressed us as individuals with high achievement and even higher aspirations, many have not yet reached their full potential. In recent years, we've noticed that more of these individuals are expressing doubt about their role as leaders. Sometimes they aren't clear about what they should be doing or where they should be heading as leaders. Some are frustrated, conflicted, or downright unhappy. Some wonder if leading is worth the time, effort, and sacrifices they have to make.

We believe doubt has increased because of the growing complexity of the leadership tasks and the interconnected world in which we live. The speed of technological developments, rate of change, economic challenges, the daily pressures to meet ever more aggressive goals, and the 24/7 access expected of leaders have left many people with too few hours and too little energy to bring their best leadership to bear. As a result, leaders have begun to question their abilities, the direction their life has taken, and their hopes for future impact. We label this as the problem of *drift*.

All of us will experience drift at some point in our lives; the authors of this book have experienced drift multiple times during their careers as leaders. As leaders or aspiring leaders, we cannot be clear about every step to take at every moment in time. The problem occurs if we stay adrift too long. Long-term drift is risky because we will make decisions by default rather than conscious choice. Being a leader requires personal enthusiasm, vision, and constant energy. If we lack these characteristics, we cause problems for ourselves and for people with whom we work.

LEADERSHIP AS A CONSCIOUS CHOICE

We wrote this book to encourage you to make conscious choices about why, when, how, and where you lead. In our experience, the ability to be clear about these choices helps you achieve greater personal success as a leader and as a person. *Discovering the Leader in You* is about helping you gain personal insight into how leadership fits in your life, the unique qualities you bring to leadership, and the impact you want to have on the world as a leader.

The book reflects our belief that many people can benefit from a conscious, systematic approach to understanding how their leadership vision, values, skills, and motivations match up with their organizational and personal realities. Our hope is to help individuals move out of states of drift and into confident action, whether they are facing a concrete leadership career decision or simply examining their reaction to an organizational change.

OUR INTENDED AUDIENCE

We believe that leadership happens at all levels in organizations, families, and communities. There are many opportunities to lead regardless of whether you hold a formal leadership position. Therefore, this revised edition of *Discovering the Leader in You* is intended to help the new employee fresh out of college, the senior executive hoping to clarify the right next step, or the volunteer working at a grassroots organization. As you will see in this book, even the most senior leaders are on a journey of clarifying who they are as leaders and discovering how to improve their effectiveness. The most effective leaders come to understand that the leadership journey is an ongoing, dynamic process without a clear beginning, middle, and end.

We hope that this book addresses the quest that many leaders have to walk a path of leadership filled with purpose and meaningful impact. We also hope it will be attractive to coaches, counselors, curriculum developers, human resource executives, and university professors, all of whom work with individuals to help them lead happier and more successful lives.

Finally, we hope this book reaches people who have not been seriously considering leadership opportunities. We believe strongly that the problems we face in the world today are largely a result of poor leadership and that the solutions to these problems will be the result of strong leadership. Leaders must not always be selected from the socio-economic elite; there's too much leadership work to be done, and it's too important to leave to a narrow cross section of the world's population.

THE DISCOVERING LEADERSHIP FRAMEWORK

This book is designed around a systematic framework that connects who you are as a leader (your vision, values, and profile) to the realities of your organizational context and the realities of your personal life. By examining the demands and expectations on you as a leader and person, you can better match your talents to the opportunities surrounding you.

The framework is based on five key topics:

1. *Current organizational realities.* The organizational context differs by individual. It can be as broad as the social, economic, and global

trends affecting leadership today. It might be more specific to your industry, your organization, or your leadership role. The goal is to understand the broader circumstances that influence your current leadership situation, as well as the demands and expectations of leaders.

2. *Leadership vision.* What is the role that leadership plays in your life? We believe that being purposeful about what you want in life is important to being purposeful about what you want as a leader. A leadership vision helps you out of drift. Without an articulate leadership vision, you will have a difficult time evaluating the leadership choices in front of you.

3. *Leadership values.* Values are the standards or principles that guide your beliefs, decisions, and actions. Understanding your values and leveraging them as a foundational cornerstone of your leadership choices is a critical contributor to effective leadership. Examining your motivations and values may give you more insight into why you feel adrift.

4. *Leadership profile.* Your leadership profile is your personal leadership tool kit and what you draw from to lead. It can include many things, such as competencies, styles, and experiences. Through careful analysis of your profile, you can assess what you see as your strengths and developmental needs. Your leadership profile further defines who you are as a leader and what you bring to leadership roles.

5. *Current personal realities.* You have a personal life that has an impact on your work life and a work life that has an impact on your personal life. Often we tend to compartmentalize these two areas of our lives when we would benefit by thinking in a more integrated and holistic way. At the end of the day, you are one person, whether you are at work, on vacation, or at home. How you integrate all aspects of your life with your responsibilities as a leader is one of the most challenging tasks you will face.

We devote a chapter to each topic of the framework. Our final chapter then guides you through a process for synthesizing data and identifying themes and patterns across the sections of the framework. This synthesis provides a valuable picture for who you are as a leader and the circumstances in which you lead best. The final step is to describe the direction you wish to go as a leader and set goals that will help you get there.

ACKNOWLEDGMENTS

All authors stand on the shoulders of those who worked the terrain before them. We acknowledge the many shoulders we have stood on to gain strength, a vision for the future, and a strong foundation to withstand the challenges that we have faced as leaders. To our colleagues at CCL, thank you for helping us along the path of our own leadership journeys.

We received wonderful support and guidance from our colleague in the CCL publications group, Peter Scisco, who gave us ideas, kept us on track, and reviewed each and every sentence we wrote. Our developmental editor extraordinaire in San Francisco, Alan Venable, took our words and sharpened their focus. Felecia Corbett in the CCL library painstakingly researched references (always with a smile on her face), and Pauline Vail at CCL helped with a number of technical aspects of putting together this book. Thanks to each of you. We also want to recognize and thank Marcia Horowitz, who was an instrumental and valuable contributor to the first edition. Without her, we wouldn't be working on this revised edition.

Most important, we thank our families who supported our disappearance for hours on end, including nights, weekends, and vacations, so that we could write this book. We couldn't have completed this book without the daily tangible and emotional support of our spouses: Craig, Judith, and Mary. We dedicate this book to our children, Thomas Chappelow, Andrew Chappelow, Ben Chappelow, Rebecca Altman, Emily Altman, David Lee, Mark Lee, and Andrea Lee and her children,

Becky and Orin Carlson-Lee. We know that the journey of discovering your own leadership paths will make the world a better place.

December 2010

Sara N. King
Greensboro, North Carolina

David G. Altman
Greensboro, North Carolina

Robert J. Lee
New York, New York

CHAPTER ONE

WHERE DOES LEADERSHIP FIT IN YOUR LIFE?

As counselors and trainers of executives and as advocates for improving the human condition through leadership development, we've noticed in recent years that increasingly more clients seem less sure about their path of leadership. Despite having had high levels of achievement and an unwavering dedication to work and career, they admit, when pressed, that something just doesn't feel right. They're uncertain about whether they're spending their best years doing what they really want to do and whether, at the end of the day, the leadership path they have chosen will ultimately be fulfilling.

This concerns us because we believe that the need for effective leadership has grown. We need strong leaders not only at the top of formal organizations (corporations, nonprofit organizations, and government agencies, for example) but also at all levels in organizations and in our communities and families. Each of us has multiple opportunities to lead every day if we choose to do so. Our hope is that in reading this book, you will find clarity about the role of leadership in your life so that you can lead more effectively in whatever situation you face.

Leadership is a hot topic, as shown by the flood of journals, books, Web sites, blogs, and training programs that now discuss what it is and how it's best practiced. Search the Web using the word *leadership*, and you will generate well over 100,000 hits. Search university offerings, and you will see classes and degrees in leadership. Pick up

1

any newspaper or news magazine, and leadership is a prominent topic covered.

Leadership can certainly be read about, studied, and taught, but individuals rarely think about leadership as a vocation, even though acquiring its skills demands the same kind of conscious decisions as acquiring a technical specialty or pursuing an educational degree. At some moment early in your life, someone may have urged you to select and develop an area of technical knowledge. But has anyone ever asked you to consider specifically how leadership would fit into your life or urge you to select and develop it as a special skill?

We wrote this book to encourage you to make more conscious choices about why, when, how, and where you lead. We think it's critical that you connect your leadership to those things you find most essential in life. Leadership is not just about developing a brilliant strategy or executing a task perfectly. We believe that the most effective leaders are those who commit themselves to getting better day by day and week by week and then apply their skills to improving the lives of other people in the organizations in which they work or their communities.

This chapter explores questions and issues that leaders like you are raising and explains how the rest of this book can help you resolve them on a personal level through structured introspection, discussion, purposeful questions, and short cases of leaders who have experienced, as television sports journalist Jim McKay used to say, "the thrill of victory and the agony of defeat." In essence, this book addresses these questions:

- Why do you want to lead?
- Who are you as a leader?
- Are your personal goals, values, needs, and resources such that your work in leadership can be both personally rewarding and outwardly fruitful?
- If you now find yourself in a leadership position or hope to be in a leadership role in the future, do you have a vision of what you'd

like your leadership work to accomplish for you personally as well as for your organization or community?
- Are you clear about when and where you are most effective as a leader?

THE CHALLENGES TODAY

Leaders must be able to cope effectively with uncertainty and continuous change. The stress, sacrifices, criticism, responsibility, and accountability that leaders face can cause us to question our roles as leaders. Some leaders we work with each week will admit that at times, they are tired, overwhelmed, stuck, lost, bored, or feeling devalued. Others aren't feeling much of anything and don't want to be noticed. Don't get us wrong: there are plenty of leaders who are optimistic and energized. But our sense is that leaders today are finding the road a bit tougher to navigate than leaders did in the past.

Leaders' New Questions

The three of us together have nearly a century of experience in assisting leaders in the development of their talents and careers. As the world becomes more interdependent and more complex, leaders with whom we work frequently come to us with questions, and sometimes concerns, about their place in the world as leaders and the place of leadership in their lives. The tenor of their questions has changed recently. Questions about strengths and developmental needs, becoming a more effective agent of change, confronting structural problems, organizational politics and difficult coworkers, and minimizing the tremendous stress of executive roles continue to surface, but they are being augmented and sometimes even replaced by a different inquiry. Contemporary leaders ask about personal and professional fulfillment, service to others, balancing the demands of work with life's other responsibilities. We hear about job dissatisfaction. We hear about job insecurity, even among the most senior leaders in organizations. Highly rated performers are not immune from having reservations about what they experience as a lack of sufficient control over both the professional and personal aspects of their careers. One corporate executive captures the confusion quite well: "It seems there have been times in your life when the options before you have seemed clouded and the trail behind you so cluttered that you can't seem to clear your feet to move ahead."

We wonder why such issues seem increasingly common. The global economic crisis that began in 2008 will no doubt affect people's perceptions of the future and their career aspirations for some time to come. Certainly the tasks of leadership in a more interdependent global world have changed from what they used to be. Advances in technology fundamentally affect the way that individuals and groups interact. When you consider how some organizations expect to have access to their leadership around the clock, getting away from work becomes quite challenging. We also wonder whether the human potential movement of the 1960s shifted people's concepts of what constitutes a happy life. Do the attitudes and expectations of the millennial generation (born between 1980 and 2000) create different expectations of leaders? When leaders demand more personal meaning in their work lives, are they responding to changes in career patterns or family relationships? In the pages that follow, we explore these and other questions leaders today are asking themselves and others.

The Problem of Drift

Some people go through life with complete clarity about their goals as a leader, but most leaders, at one point or another, express doubts about their capabilities, have questions about how best to leverage their talents, or are simply confused about the leader within them. We call this the problem of *drift*. Drift can feel as if you are going through the motions but not actually moving forward. It can be short-lived (for instance, after a challenging meeting or a tough week, you may begin to wonder whether you can handle the expectations of your team) or it can be chronic (for example, after five years in a job, you realize that unless you make a change, some of your life's goals are not going to be met).

Think of drift as being opposite to being "in the zone," or in a place in life in which you are making conscious choices and taking action with a clear sense of purpose and connection to your core values and goals.

We work with leaders in all kinds of organizations, from multinational to grassroots and from public to private sector. Drift is an equal opportunity employer that at some point affects leaders from all walks of life. Whether underqualified, underchallenged, overwhelmed, burned out, or in some other way miscast, it's not uncommon for leaders to feel out of place in their current roles, unprepared for the demands of leadership, misaligned with their responsibilities, unaware of the unknown factors inherent in a leadership role, or unsure about how to seize the potential for change and get back on the right track. One goal of this book is to help you address issues you may have about drift and about your sense of focus, purpose, effectiveness, and drive as a leader. We will help you move from feeling a sense of drift to a place where you reach your full potential as a leader by delineating a process of discovering the leader in you.

Drift can occur for a number of reasons. Consider these situations, and see if any are familiar to you:

- *You are overwhelmed.* Your organization let go of 15 percent of its workforce. You are now covering the leadership responsibilities for three departments. How can you be effective with so much responsibility?
- *You are skeptical.* Your organization has undergone the third major restructuring in three years. Change is the name of the game, but to what end isn't clear. You are responsible for motivating your team and getting them on board with the changes. How can you do that when you don't believe in the change yourself?
- *You are stuck.* You have been doing the same job for the past four years. Because of your organization's outsourcing to overseas locations, moving to a new position would require you to move abroad. You see little opportunity for advancement given your desire to stay rooted in your community. Your work is critical to

the organization's success, but the fire in your belly is not as strong as it once was. How do you get excited again?

- *You are lost.* Your boss and three other senior leaders have left the organization. You are being asked to fill in on some of their key projects, while others in the organization conduct a search to fill these positions. You didn't want more responsibility, but others are looking to you for answers. How do you step up to the plate when you're not sure you can swing the bat, let alone hit the pitch?

- *You are in denial.* You have had six bosses in three years. Change keeps coming, but you don't know what is going to ultimately stick. Perhaps if you ignore the newest change, hunker down, and pretend to be onboard, this too shall pass. How long can you wait?

- *You are angry.* Your spouse lost her job, and the job market in your area is horrendous. You have decided to move, but you love your organization, your role, and your colleagues. How will you find the right next leadership role?

- *You are unhappy.* You have often made leadership and career decisions based on the expectations of others. You chose your field because of your father's encouragement. You said yes to each organizational opportunity because your boss, mentor, or spouse said it was the right thing to do. But now you realize you aren't doing what you want to do. How do you break the cycle and find a job that is more connected to your core values?

- *You are pressured.* In order to put your three children through college, maintain your financial commitments to nonprofit organizations you care about, and contribute to your own retirement account, you feel pressure to serve in a high-level, well-paying position where the perks and financial rewards are plentiful. How do you find respite from the demands of the role?

- *You are underchallenged.* You are twenty-seven years old and new to the organization. You believe that you have a lot to give, and yet your boss continues to ask you to work on routine tasks you mastered several years ago. You see many opportunities to lead, but your boss seems threatened by giving you too much exposure. How do you convince her that you are ready for more?

- *You are worried.* You have been asked to volunteer your time on a major cross-functional taskforce with high visibility. You have just had your first child and learning how to manage the role of parent, spouse, and employee. You are already finding it difficult to keep up with all of the demands in your life. How can you add still more work to your plate?

- *You are thrilled.* You have just landed the marketing job you always wanted: leading a project team for one of your firm's major accounts. But this is your first real leadership role, and you are unsure of how to best organize, lead, and motivate your team. Is there a map to help guide your next steps?

- *You are nervous.* You are the first expatriate for the company and are moving your entire family to Hong Kong. You will be charting new territory by opening the first office in Asia and leading a culturally diverse workforce. You are not sure what to do next. Instead of taking action, you feel stuck in place, almost paralyzed. What do you do first?

These situations describe the multitude of questions that leaders at all levels are asking. Given the pace of change in organizations, individuals who are in a pretty good place can suddenly find themselves thrust into situations they didn't foresee or don't know how to handle. These situations have both a professional and personal impact on them.

We have had many conversations with clients who faced one or more of these issues. Our conversations revealed that many leaders find themselves in the middle of situations and don't have a systematic way to navigate to a better place. All in all, they haven't conducted much of a conscious, guided evaluation of themselves as leaders. Intrigued by drift, we probed further by asking, Have you thought about the role that leadership plays in your life? Has leadership been a conscious decision? In a few cases, the answers were a resounding yes; the individuals had indeed given much thought to who they were as leaders and the skills they wanted to develop in the future. These individuals came across as self-assured. Some planned to move up to the next level, and a few were content to end their careers in the jobs they held. In either case, they stood on solid ground. But most of the leaders we talked with hadn't been very thoughtful about assuming a leadership position. One leader described "falling into" his position. Another said, "I don't even give it a second thought. You know, it's like you just try to get through each day and do the best you can."

These conversations, no matter the amount of change or circumstances, confirm our belief that too few individuals actively think about leadership or are truly comfortable with their identities as leaders. We are struck by how seldom people in leadership positions consider to any great extent their work as leaders. We are well acquainted with people who are so keen on assuming leadership responsibilities that they have pursued that goal without paying enough attention to the meaning of the work or the fact that developing others was a critical skill for being a successful leader. Not only are individuals uncomfortable with their identities as leaders, more are walking the halls of organizations disillusioned, dissatisfied, and disconnected. Rather than being active in tackling the issues before them, they hide out in their offices, work from home, disassociate themselves from mistakes, and hunker down hoping that this too shall pass. The main question they ask is, "Is taking this leadership role worth the effort?"

The bad news is that the problem of drift has impact beyond individual discomfort. Since leadership is about having responsibility for others, drift has consequences that can be challenging and frustrating for colleagues and families as well. Leading by rote wastes good talent and energy, dilutes the talent and energy that others muster to create results, and creates drag on company resources. Perhaps worse, while in the grip of drift, you can experience a malaise that stands in the way of full commitment and fulfillment. This malaise can be contagious and infect other members of your team or work group.

If you feel this way, be comforted by the fact that many others do as well. Do you want help moving out of the drift cycle? If you do, you will benefit by stepping back, asking yourself some fundamental questions, and then figuring out how to get back in the driver's seat. The process can help you gain traction for moving yourself to a place of fulfillment, commitment, and motivation.

Reflect on the following questions, and write down responses that immediately come to mind:

- How much of your life today involves being a leader? (Don't limit your answer to just your work life.)
- Are you currently in a leadership role? How did you get there?
- Do you see yourself as a leader? Are you a leader all of the time?
- How comfortable are you with your identity as a leader?
- Did you choose to become a leader, or did it somehow choose you?

By answering these and other questions we pose throughout this book, you will be making the decision and commitment to move away from drift. Deane Shapiro wrote in *Precision Nirvana*, "When sitting just sit. When walking just walk. Above all don't wobble" (1978, p. 149). We believe this is good advice to you, and we add this corollary: When leading, lead; when following, follow; but take action always.

FROM DRIFT TO CLARITY: A FRAMEWORK FOR CHOICE AND ACTION

Many people who are in or are considering leadership roles can benefit from a systematic look at themselves as leaders. By paying attention to all the different aspects of leading, you might gain useful insight into your short-term situations and long-term plans.

Choosing Leadership

Demands for leadership come in many guises and are not always clearly signaled by job title, job description, or status. For example, a researcher discovers that her position involves interacting with clients who are using products that the researcher has studied. When she realizes that her research will have more value if she gets out of the lab and sees how customers actually use those products, she leads a revision of her organization's research protocols. Or a senior graphic designer realizes that he spends more time attempting to inspire good work from freelance artists from all over the globe than he spends creating images of his own. Collaborating with these artists requires a deep knowledge of culture and context. The designer needs to develop skills around leading a charge to break down the barriers between in-house and outsourced talent. Or a community organizer working at a nonprofit has to tap into the collective capabilities of local citizens, and in the process she helps to build a community's capacity to address poverty.

In other words, at all levels in an organization, individuals can and do become leaders. Sometimes they explicitly and intentionally step forward to take on a leadership role; sometimes they are asked to do so; sometimes the leadership blossoms organically from their daily practices. Even if you are not designated with a formal title (for example, you don't have a manager title or you don't supervise a staff), if you pay attention and build your self-awareness, you can daily discover opportunities to lead.

The Discovering Leadership Framework

Knowing that most current and prospective leaders had never systematically looked at the situation they find themselves in and tried a more integrated approach to their solutions, we developed the Discovering Leadership Framework (Figure 1.1). Its purpose is to help you better see the role of leadership in your life. It will help you reach the point of saying, "This is the perfect role for me," "I am just not suited to this work," "This is how I can lead more effectively," or "Yes, this is why I lead."

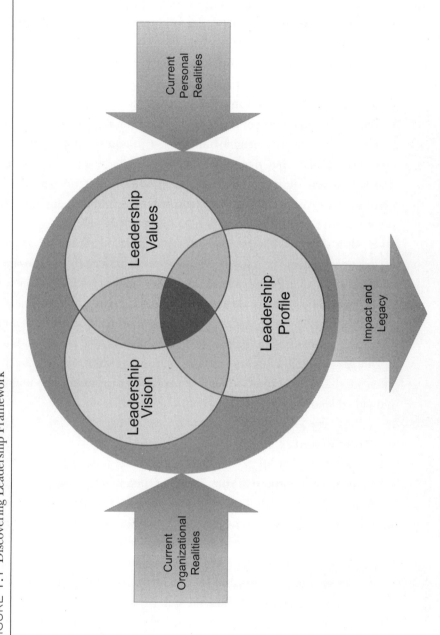

FIGURE 1.1 Discovering Leadership Framework

The five areas of the framework will help you organize your thinking by logically connecting important career and life issues with leadership development activities:

Current Organizational Realities

The problem of drift and what leadership opportunities are available to us is always embedded in a larger context. This context differs by individual. It can be as broad as the social, economic, and global trends that have an impact on leadership today. It might be more specific to your industry. Is it one of growth (the energy industry) or one of decline (the U.S. textile industry)? It might be specific to your organization if there are structural changes, cutbacks, or new ventures. It might be the context of your current or potential leadership role. Do you have a new boss or a difficult employee? Organizational culture and climate are part of your context as well. The point is to understand the broader circumstances that define your leadership situation and why you feel adrift. Context also refers to the new demands and expectations leaders face, the main views of leadership in your organization, and their fit with your own view or philosophy. We have included the costs of leading as part of the organizational context. We know these costs are often specific to the organization, role, and other circumstances that an individual leader faces.

Your Vision

A vision for your life is your ideal future state. It describes what you see as the overall purpose of your life: what dreams you want to achieve, what goals you want to accomplish, the people you want to be with, and the kind of life you want to have. This framework takes a specific look at your leadership vision. More specifically, what is the role that leadership plays in your life? We believe that being purposeful about what you want in life is important to being purposeful about what you want in your leadership situation. A leadership vision helps you out of drift. Without an articulate leadership vision, you will have a difficult time evaluating the leadership choices presented to you.

Your Values

Values are the standards or principles that guide your beliefs, decisions, and actions. Understanding your values and leveraging them as a foundational cornerstone of your leadership choices is a critical contributor to effective leadership. Articulating your motivations and values and understanding their role in your work as a leader isn't an easy task. Neither is figuring out if your motivations and values align with your current role or with your organization's values. Examining your motivations and values may give you more insight into why you feel adrift.

Your Leadership Profile

Your leadership profile is your personal leadership tool kit and what you draw from to lead. It can include many things, such as competencies, styles, and experiences. Through careful analysis of your profile, you can identify what you see as your strengths and developmental needs. Your leadership profile further defines who you are as a leader and what you bring to leadership roles. Knowing your profile helps you clarify why and how you lead, why you might be adrift, and how to take action to move in a more positive direction.

Personal Realities and Expectations

You have a personal life that has an impact on your work life and a work life that has an impact on your personal life. Often we tend to compartmentalize these two areas of our lives when we would benefit by thinking in a more integrated and holistic way. At the end of the day, you are one person, whether you are at work, on vacation, or at home. How you integrate all aspects of your life with your responsibilities as a leader is one of the most challenging that you will face.

These five areas of the framework are closely related. Our goal in presenting this framework is to help you make more conscious, unifying connections that will help you move from drift into clarity.

THE UNDERLYING PHILOSOPHY OF DISCOVERING LEADERSHIP

As authors, we share a belief that individuals should choose fulfilling, meaningful work that they are passionate about. What is it that you really want to do? This is a key question to discovering the leader in you. If you are not doing what is meaningful to you, think hard about whether you need to find something else to do. In *Man's Search for Meaning* (1959), Viktor Frankl observed that a life without purpose is a life full of pain and hardship. Thus, one of the most important tasks for a leader is to find an anchor point of deep purpose and to draw on that anchor point during good and bad times.

Consider what Steve Jobs, the CEO of Apple, told the Stanford University graduating class of 2005. Given the success of Jobs and the innovative industrial designs that flow out of Apple Computer, you might expect a speech about creativity, about pushing limits, about looking beyond the horizon. But the core of his commencement address was about the utter importance of loving what you do, even when times are challenging:

> I found what I loved to do early in life. Woz [Steve Wozniak] and I started Apple in my parents' garage when I was 20. We worked hard, and in 10 years Apple had grown from just the two of us in a garage into a $2 billion company with over 4000 employees. We had just released our finest creation—the Macintosh—a year earlier, and I had just turned 30. And then I got fired. . . . What had been the focus of my entire adult life was gone, and it was devastating.
>
> . . . I didn't see it then, but it turned out that getting fired from Apple was the best thing that could have ever happened to me. The heaviness of being successful was replaced by the lightness of being a beginner again, less sure about everything. It freed me to enter one of the most creative periods of my life.
>
> During the next five years, I started a company named NeXT, another company named Pixar, and fell in love with an amazing

woman who would become my wife. Pixar went on to create the world's first computer animated feature film, *Toy Story*, and is now the most successful animation studio in the world. In a remarkable turn of events, Apple bought NeXT, I returned to Apple, and the technology we developed at NeXT is at the heart of Apple's current renaissance. And Laurene and I have a wonderful family together.

I'm pretty sure none of this would have happened if I hadn't been fired from Apple. . . . I'm convinced that the only thing that kept me going was that I loved what I did. You've got to find what you love. And that is as true for your work as it is for your lovers. Your work is going to fill a large part of your life, and the only way to be truly satisfied is to do what you believe is great work. And the only way to do great work is to love what you do. If you haven't found it yet, keep looking. Don't settle. As with all matters of the heart, you'll know when you find it. And, like any great relationship, it just gets better and better as the years roll on. So keep looking until you find it. Don't settle ["You've Got to Find What You Love," 2005].

Jobs's advice is as relevant to individuals who are well into their careers as it is to newly minted graduates. Without meaning, creative leadership can't flourish.

Even if you do discover what you really want to do as a leader, leading is still hard work, and it comes with both pleasure and pain. Discovering the leader in you is not for the faint of heart. It requires deep introspection about what is important in your life, what you would like to pursue as your legacy, and whether you are willing to genuinely seek and act on feedback from others.

Peter Drucker often encouraged people to think about their legacy. He suggested that if you don't know what you want to be remembered for by the age of fifty, it's doubtful that you will leave much of a positive legacy (2001). To discover the leader in you requires that you regularly evaluate what you want to contribute in life. Drucker argued that considering this question is one of the best ways for you to renew and reinvent yourself. Don't put this off until late in your career. Even if you are just starting out on your leadership journey, set aside time each year to evaluate the larger question of legacy. If you keep this in the front of your mind, year in and year out, you'll have a better chance of fulfilling your true potential.

We believe that leadership can be learned, that self-awareness is critical to leadership development, and that people can learn, grow, and change so that they can become the kind of leader needed for the context in which they live and work. That's not to say that everyone can develop or needs to develop into great leaders. But most great leaders are great because they take the time to learn, grow, and get better; in other words, they are made, not born.

Our philosophy and approach resonate with the work on mind-set by Carol Dweck and her colleagues at Stanford University. Consider that scientists used to think that personality and intelligence were hardwired (fixed) at a very early age. We now know from a large body of research that while all humans have some hardwired characteristics and abilities, their capabilities and skills are not predetermined. Those attributes are heavily influenced by the perceptions that people have of themselves, the actions that they take, their life experiences, and the contexts in which they have lived (Dweck, 2006; McAdams, 2006). Dweck (2006) writes about the importance of having a growth mind-set (a belief that your skills and effectiveness are malleable by cultivation and practice). People with a growth mind-set "believe that a person's true potential is unknown (and unknowable); that it's impossible to foresee what can be accomplished with years of passion, toil, and training" (p. 7). Dweck has shown that managers who have a growth mind-set appreciate talent but do not rely on talent alone to ensure that their employees are effective. Instead, these managers invest in developmental conversations, coaching, mentoring, and other interventions to ensure that their employees become more effective and don't remain stuck. The idea that one's potential is never known and continual investment in acquiring knowledge and skills can lead to more effective leadership is an empowering one.

It's unrealistic to think that you can develop a high-powered growth mind-set overnight. Rather, view the development or nurturing of this mind-set as a marathon rather than a sprint. You can best develop your leadership skills by deconstructing big developmental challenges into smaller, more manageable chunks. Small changes in your behavior accumulate over time and can lead to substantial, substantive change.

In short, leadership must take on meaning, and you have to define its significance to you. You must also focus on developing the skills that you believe are important to help you address your goals. To do this, you must believe that you can improve, and you must have deep self-awareness of what to work on to produce the greatest gains in leadership abilities.

EVERYDAY, EVERYWHERE LEADERSHIP

Although the leaders we counsel speak about their roles in terms of their jobs and careers, few spontaneously consider leadership roles away from the office—as a parent, a community volunteer, a fundraiser, a political campaign worker, or a club member, for example. The next time someone asks, "What do you do?" think about this: Embedded in that question are assumptions about social status, economic success, and individual power. Defy those assumptions and your own expectation that the person asking the question wants to hear only about your work. Talk about your interests, your mission in life, or some topic other than your job. Reclaim what defines you as a person (not what's on your business card) and what you hope to accomplish in your life (not the business goals you're responsible for completing by the end of the quarter).

Although this book focuses primarily on questions of leadership at work, we urge you to think about leadership opportunities outside your own organization. Many of the ideas in this book carry over to non-job-related leadership. A leadership role in family and community situations allows you to try new skills, styles, and levels of responsibility. Such opportunities often allow more flexibility in terms of the length of time you hold a leading role and how long you choose to do so. For some people, the best expression of their values may be to remain individual contributors at work and leaders in a nonwork setting.

Whether in an organization or in less formal situations, you can gain greater understanding and mastery of your leadership potential and practice with systematic self-assessment. You can also overcome some of the passivity that perhaps has led you into a position of leadership that you never made a decision to enter and where you may now feel less than fulfilled. If leadership opportunities are important to you (and given the need for leadership around the world in all kinds of situations, we hope that they are), you'll benefit by becoming more aware of how your personal vision, goals, and other aspects of your life can enhance or direct your choices. You can master and enjoy a life filled with leadership, as you choose it.

WHAT'S NEXT

Each of the next five chapters covers one component of the Discovering Leadership Framework. Chapter Two asks what you see happening in the turbulent world of organizations, what impact those changes have on leadership, and what forces are shaping your current feelings about being a leader. Do those forces present opportunities for you to develop as a leader?

Chapter Three explores the important role that leadership vision plays in effective leadership. Do you work from a vision that provides meaning, purpose, energy, and passion to yourself and others and how does your leadership vision connect to who you are as person?

Chapter Four asks you to assess your motivations and values to see how they are reflected in your life and how strongly they serve as a basis for leadership. This analysis will help you uncover conflicts or disconnects that might interfere with your leadership work.

Chapter Five is about your awareness of your own particular skills and qualities related to leadership. It leads you through an inventory of your own leadership competencies, roles, learning styles, and knowledge. It will help you pinpoint talents and skills where you show strength and others where you may want to improve.

Chapter Six considers the impact of a leadership role on the other aspects of your life. It suggests ways in which your life at home and at work can be more mutually integrated and supportive.

Chapter Seven brings you back to the Discovering the Leadership Framework and helps you identify themes and patterns among the various components of the framework. From this analysis we hope that you gain more clarity about why, how, when, and where you lead.

CHAPTER TWO

ORGANIZATIONAL REALITIES, DEMANDS, AND EXPECTATIONS

In Chapter One, we described a number of situations that raise questions in the minds of leaders. Many of these come about because of changes that organizations face. Reductions in force, restructuring, changes in a boss, loss of a job, and new job opportunities all affect leaders. Many of these organizational changes result from external forces such as greater competition, loss of revenue, or other economic forces. All of these changes affect what leadership opportunities are available to you, the nature of the opportunities, the challenges they bring, the kind of leader you want to be, and what you can accomplish. These changes also influence how leaders are expected to act, be, show up, and lead.

These issues often cause some leaders to ask, "Is being a leader worth it?" Unrealistic expectations or criticism from others can leave you paralyzed or drifting. Perhaps your team expected you to be a heroic figure and save the organization or to continue driving the mission like the former senior leadership team. But is that (and its costs) what you had in mind?

Thus, the first step toward discovering the leader in you is to gain more understanding of your personal leadership situation. To aid your thinking, this chapter briefly describes recent trends in organizational life. It explores the impact of organizational life on current expectations of leaders, leaders' own expanding views of leadership, and perceived costs of leading. Reviewing this part of the leadership framework should give you insights into why you are adrift and possible steps and choices that can help you get out of drift.

HOW ORGANIZATIONS AND ORGANIZATIONAL LIFE ARE CHANGING

We can no longer define organizations as clearly as we once could. Many have become so diffuse and pluralistic that static models like command-and-control hierarchies and interrelated systems (organic or machine) are no longer as relevant. Back in 1995, management guru Peter Drucker portrayed organizations as inherently unstable because they "must be attuned for innovation, for the systematic abandonment of whatever is established, customary, familiar, and comfortable" (p. 77). Today the external environment continues to change constantly, and so too must organizations and their leaders.

In 2007, CCL researchers published survey data from nearly four hundred participants in CCL's Leadership Development Program. A little over half were from the United States, and most held middle or upper management positions. Most (84 percent) said the definition of effective leadership had changed in the past five years. When asked how, respondents mentioned needing more flexible, cross-boundary, collaborative, and collective leadership skill sets. Were we to repeat this survey in five years, a few new factors would likely emerge. The point is that to be effective as a leader, you must be a student of the contexts in which you lead and develop or refine your leadership skills to meet new demands.

We've all heard the story about the buggy whip industry in the early twentieth century, about the time when automobiles entered the marketplace. Some buggy whip companies thought that they were in the business of making buggy whips. Others realized that they were part of the transportation industry. Most of the former went out of business since buggy whips were not all that useful in getting autos moving down the road. Those who understood that they were in the transportation industry stayed in business, albeit with different products and business models. Most leaders these days are like the buggy whip manufacturers of one hundred years ago. It's easy to become a disengaged, out-of-touch leader, knowing that you have to change but acting along the lines of a common definition of *insanity:* doing the same thing over and over and expecting a different outcome. If you pay keen, multisensory attention to the changing context inside and outside your organization, in your private and your public life, and you adapt to the challenges and opportunities change brings, then your leadership effectiveness will grow. It requires using all of your senses, and it's not easy work, since what's happening around you is often not clear.

Let's take a look now at some broad contextual factors that affect organizational life today and the changing requirements of leaders worldwide:

- The current organization-customer relationship
- The changing definition of careers and work
- Diversification of the workforce
- The rise of globalized organizations
- Technological innovations

If these factors don't fully capture your reality, take a moment to identify additional ones that are important to you and the context in which you lead.

Changes in How Organizations and Customers Connect

Many years ago when flappers danced the Charleston and what was good for General Motors was good for America, status and hierarchy were understood and accepted as primary qualities of organizations. This time of innocence was marked by a common understanding of assets, ownership, employees, bosses, and customers. Distinctions among roles were clear and accepted. Organizations owned or controlled whatever they considered their business. Efficiency was a question of continuous high levels of production and sales that pushed volume beyond a fixed break-even point: the greater the volume, the greater the profitability. Customers were on the receiving end of organizational outputs or products, and customization for the customer was not a part of the organizational lexicon.

But change was in the air even then. Technological advances led to continuous change, faster communication, and new product lines. Products became more sophisticated. More assets became intellectual than physical. And customers began to have a direct influence on the future plans of organizations.

Today the Internet provides customers with knowledge, power, and access to competitors' products and the ability to rate the quality of products for everyone to see. Buyers expect more for their money and will cross whatever oceans, deserts, or Web pages may be necessary to find the right product or service. They need no longer walk into stores or drive to distant malls. Because customers now demand customization, product and service options have multiplied.

In response, organizations now strive for highly competitive, quality- and cost-conscious environments where flexibility and responsiveness are paramount. Rapid cycle time is now seen as a major source of competitive advantage, and the norm is to have the next version of a product gearing up before the last one has fully rolled out. Innovation, entrepreneurial ventures, and new distribution channels are the name of the game.

Structurally many organizations are moving from primarily hierarchical structures to collective forms to meet customer needs anywhere and at any time. This often causes a movement toward decentralization or regionalization. A competing force or tension is that in order to grow, large organizations must acquire smaller ones or establish key partnerships if they want their business to grow. Growing in size often leads to centralization of services, yet at the same time, dispersal of authority and expertise and a decentralization of power are necessary to meet customer needs.

In light of these changes, think about the following questions:

- How have increased customer demands affected your organization and your role as a leader?
- How has your organization responded to dynamic changes in the broader marketplace, and what are the implications of these changes for leadership needs in your organization?
- What structural or role changes have taken place in your organization in response to customer demands?
- What differences have these changes made to your relationships with peers, your boss, and people who work for you?
- Have any of these changes left you adrift? In what ways?

Changes in the Definitions of Career and Work

As authority disperses and organizational structures alter, employment arrangements have also changed. Employees are increasingly likely to change jobs and organizations many times over their career. The proverbial gold watch for "lifers" is now rare. Organizations no longer have the obligation or desire to employ everyone full time. Increasingly, organizations are using temporary, part-time, flexible, partnered, telecommuting, outsourced, and interim manager roles. By such arrangements organizations manage particular risks, such as avoiding the high cost of layoffs in a downturn yet preserve the labor they need to respond to peaks or emergencies. Role flexibility and fiscal responsibility become paramount in workforce strategies.

Such changes can fracture engagement and loyalty if they are not managed carefully. Keeping a disconnected and temporary workforce engaged, focused, loyal, and committed is not an easy leadership task. Finding common motivations and purpose is more difficult. When employers spend more time managing risk and less time valuing employees, loyalty diminishes on both ends. Resulting higher turnover can be costly to employers and compromise customer service when organizational knowledge walks out the door.

These employment changes have triggered new orientations to jobs and careers, with a greater emphasis on tasks and assignments and less on ongoing jobs. Increasingly, although workers perform tasks, they also need to create their own tasks to become more entrepreneurial. The location of work is also shifting, from brick-and-mortar sites to networks spanning oceans. More people work from home, on planes, in hotel rooms, and in other settings. More people are "vendor-minded" temporary workers, looking for unmet needs to which they can apply their skills, and interacting with peers, bosses, customers, clients, and organizations through social networks. In short, how future work gets done and who is involved will largely be up to individuals who are managing their own negotiations, not by traditional organizational decision-making structures using traditional work processes.

Think about the following:

- What has been the impact of this new orientation to work and careers on you?
- How has it changed the way you lead and the pressing leadership challenges you face?
- How can you better manage your own career?
- What strategies can you and other leaders use to increase engagement and commitment around the work?
- What can you do to maintain your own commitment and engagement?

Leading a More Diverse Workforce

Over the past several decades, the workforce has diversified dramatically. Research and discussions in workplaces and at home proliferate about trends: the aging baby boomer generation on the brink of retirement; the presence and impact of Generations X and Y and the millennials; the increase in the number of women in the labor force; and the increase in Hispanic/Latino, African American, and Asian workers.

Attracting and retaining a diverse workforce has become a business financial imperative, from having enough of the right resources to understanding the increasingly diverse customer pool in order to provide the right products and services. In James Canton's (2006) list of the top ten workforce trends for 2009, six of the ten relate to global talent, the aging population, women, and broader diversity issues. Understanding, attracting, retaining, leading, and engaging a diverse workforce have never before been more important.

How do these trends relate to drift? As a member of the workforce, we all want to be valued and understood. Drift may be a result of not feeling valued or not finding the right fit within an organization or with an entrepreneurial venture. It might be the result of not feeling that you have sufficient power or influence over your own career choices. Drift might also result from uncertainty in how to motivate and retain individuals who are different from you. Reflect on how the factors discussed below bear on you and your leadership situation as it relates to drift or to the process of discovering the leader in you.

Generational Diversity

Considerable attention is given today to the number of generations working side by side in organizations, and it's commonly assumed that major differences between generations cause conflict and dissatisfaction in the workplace. In particular, a common stereotype is that the younger generations (for example, Gen X, born between the mid-1960s and the late 1970s, and Gen Y, born between 1980 and 2000) are very different from each other and from earlier generations (baby boomers and the silent generation). Despite the common notion that generations are fundamentally different, Jennifer Deal (2007) argues that there are more similarities than differences between generations, especially in the area of personal values such as family, integrity, achievement, love, competence, and happiness. Why is the belief that different generations have different values so prevalent? Why do so many of us extrapolate from that belief that it's difficult for leaders to create cohesion among teams and work groups composed of differently aged workers, and that it's difficult for young and old workers to get along at work? Deal explains that the differences are found in how people of different generations act on those values, not in the values themselves. When one group of people acts differently from another group, people of either group make faulty attributions about the causes of behavioral differences and often blame different values rather than chalking it up to the different ways people have for interacting with the world.

While people of different generations behave somewhat differently (especially when it comes to communication or the use of technology), many underlying values, beliefs, and aspirations are more similar than dissimilar. Generational conflict in the workplace is more likely due to issues of control, power, and authority than to more fundamental problems. As Deal (2007) argues, a lot of the conflict experienced at work emerges in struggles of authority and power, which are often exacerbated between older and younger workers: younger managers seek authority and power, and older managers often want to maintain the authority and power they have built over the years. We could reach the same conclusion about differences of race, socioeconomic status, or other such factors. Many so-called differences come down to power, control, and authority. A perceived lack of power, control, and authority can often lead to drift when it creates a sense of not feeling valued or not finding the right fit with an organization.

Do generational issues play a part of the context of your leadership? If part of your current organizational context labels you as a member of a younger generation than the current leadership and so detracts from your being taken seriously, how might you reframe the situation and make different attributions about the values and beliefs of older generations? If you lead multiple generations, how can you lead differently? If you are managing a person twenty years older than you, how might you better bridge any misunderstandings or conflict?

Gender Diversity

If generational issues don't have an impact on you as an individual or leader, gender issues might. For many years, research, articles, programs, and informal discussions have focused on a number of gender questions. Why don't more women hold the top positions in organizations? Do men and women lead differently? Are men or women seen as more effective leaders? Do women and men bring different communication styles to organizations? Why do fewer women than men occupy line positions? What impact do different cultural attitudes toward men and women have on leadership practice and potential? These and other questions have led individuals and organizations to examine their assumptions, beliefs, policies, and practices about both men and women in the workforce.

In the United States, statistics related to gender have changed dramatically over the past five decades. For example, Gail Collins (2009) notes that in the early 1960s, "women were vigorously discouraged from seeking jobs that men might have wanted" (2009, p. 20). She compares that sentiment to today, when women claim almost half of the seats in U.S. medical and law schools. These trends continue: more women than ever before are enlisting in the military, becoming engineers, and starting their own companies.

Another data trend shows that in the 2008 economic recession, more men than women lost their jobs. This is due in part to more women than men in part-time positions and in lower-paying jobs. However, women now make up over 50 percent of the labor pool and are being recognized as strong consumers in the marketplace. Women make purchasing decisions on 94 percent of home furnishings, 92 percent of vacations, 91 percent of homes, 60 percent of automobiles, and 51 percent of electronics (Silverstein and Sayre, 2009). Organizations now look to their female employees for product and service ideas to attract this consumer base.

In addition, more research studies conducted in the United States have reported the positive financial contributions that women make in the workplace (see, for example, Desvaux, Devillard-Hoellinger, and Meaney, 2008; Shipman and Kay, 2009). All of these forces have led Heather Boushey and Ann O'Leary, the authors of *The Shriver Report* (2009), to identify the coming decade as one of transformation comparable to the age of industrialization, the civil rights movement, and the creation of the Internet.

What is the effect of these trends in organizations? Some women are finding their way to more senior levels in organizations. Some are leaving to start their own companies. Some are achieving equal pay for equal work, but many are not. Some are leading the charge for more flexible work arrangements. And others are facing challenges related to leadership choices as they address their own questions: Where do I best fit? Can I balance the responsibilities of a demanding leadership role and family responsibilities? Can I break into an established network?

Men are not immune to these same challenges, and they certainly experience drift and uncertainty in considering themselves as leaders and how they might lead. They are also choosing to start their own businesses or work part time; others, due to the economy, are being forced to change their work hours, become the stay-at-home spouse, or make other career choices that they had never before envisioned. Both men and women encounter gender differences, stereotypes, and bias. Because of these changes in how both men and women work, negotiation increases at home over family schedules, household chores, and travel conflicts.

All of these changes affect organizations, leaders, and individuals. How do leaders ensure that they have the right talent, whether men or women, in their organizations? How can leaders combat gender bias and stereotypes? How do gender issues at work and at home affect you? How might this dynamic contribute to or inhibit discovering the leader in you?

Cultural Diversity

With changing demographics and a more globally connected world, diverse cultures have proliferated in our schools, communities, neighborhoods, religious institutions, and organizations. As the world gets smaller, we experience differences in traditions, communication patterns, language, personal space, consumer habits, humor, orientation to time, attitudes toward work, responses to authority, family expectations, expressions of identity, norms, how knowledge is acquired, and responses to change. These differences have changed how employees interact with bosses, how teams work together, how groups communicate across geographical distances, how work gets done, and how conflict gets dealt with or not, and how leaders need to engage a diverse workforce. Cultural diversity also affects how well the supply chain works, how global partnerships succeed or fail, and how governments determine new policies. What does it mean for all members of a workforce to feel valued and appreciated? What members of a diverse culture might be more prone to drift? How does this trend affect you, and in what way might it contribute to your feelings of drift?

Now think about the following questions and how all of the changing demographics of your workforce affect your role now and in the future as a leader:

- How would you describe the changing diversity in your organization (generational, gender, ethnic, cultural)? What impact is it having?
- What do you anticipate as further changes around diversity that will arise in the next five years?
- How is your organization taking advantage of the new workforce playing field in order to be more competitive?
- How might these trends be connected to your challenges or feelings of drift as a leader?
- In various respects, how would you describe your status as minority or majority? How might that status influence your behaviors or your feelings of value as a leader?
- As you look forward five years, what skill sets and worldviews do you need to develop to be a more effective leader in an increasingly diverse world?

Globalization

Is the world indeed flat, as Thomas Friedman (2005) claims? He argues that technology innovations allow individuals and organizations around the world to grasp unprecedented opportunities by reducing the obstacles to labor, resources, and markets to the same level for every organization. But when Richard Florida (2005) examined global economic data, he reached a different conclusion. He argues that the world is spiky, full of growing disparities and inequities (peaks and valleys) that vary across populations and geographies. Indeed, he found that although more people were living in urban areas than at any other time in the world's history, the economic output of the world's largest cities varied greatly. He also found that by various measures of innovation, there are tremendous differences across regions, countries, and cities. For example, in 2002, 85 percent of the patents granted came from just five countries: the United States, Japan, South Korea, Germany, and Russia. Whether seen as flat or spiky, the world is more connected than ever before because of technology and communication developments that create more opportunities to lead growth.

The global recession beginning in 2008 illustrates the tight connections among economies of different countries and different organizations. When businesses and nonprofit services in the United States suffer an economic downturn, small and large countries around the world feel that pain. In November 2009, for example, after years of explosive growth in Dubai, the global economic recession caused massive debt, and the country struggled to pay off loans. Its request for a six-month reprieve on its bills caused an immediate drop on world markets and led neighboring Abu Dhabi to provide significant economic assistance. Likewise, when a single, large multinational company goes out of business or into bankruptcy, as Lehman Brothers and General Motors did, the reverberations are felt far and wide.

The rise of globally connected companies causes many leaders to talk about the challenges they face in working across time zones and cultures, ranging from the mundane (such as finding a suitable time for a conference call involving people from different countries) to the critical and complex (cultural differences that can derail a project because of miscommunication or misperceptions). Global connections have also led to more opportunities to live abroad and take on the challenges of expatriation.

In 2008 and 2009, CCL researchers asked senior executives who participated in its Leadership at the Peak program about such boundary-spanning challenges. Most of these leaders (86 percent) reported that it was extremely important for them to work effectively across boundaries in their current leadership role. They needed new leadership skills to address problems at the intersections of all kinds of organizational, cultural, demographic, and geographical boundaries. Leaders increasingly realize that they need to operate beyond the boxes and lines of the organizational chart. Yet only 7 percent of those whom CCL surveyed believed they were very effective at it (Ernst and Yip, 2008).

Think about the impact of globalization on you and your organization:

- Does your organization have a global reach? What leadership opportunities are available to you beyond where you live? If you lived in a different city or country, how would that affect your future effectiveness as a leader?
- What is the impact of globalization on your leadership? Compared to five years ago, do you have more or fewer boundary-spanning tasks?
- What challenges do you face working across time zones, geographies, cultures, or religions?
- How does the complexity of working globally and across boundaries contribute (or not) to feelings of drift?

Technology and Other Innovations

Technological innovations give individuals unprecedented global access to people and information. Technology has also led people to work more synchronously (through teleconferences, Web meetings, and the like) and asynchronously 24/7 (by e-mail, recorded Web-based presentations, and such). Smartphones, mobile phones, and a host of digital accessories connect more and more of us to colleagues, reports, and customers at all times and in all places. Disconnecting from work, even for a few hours, now takes a conscious effort.

Technological changes have been profound and continuous. In response, organizations look to instill a culture of innovation in order to compete more effectively in an ever changing environment. Pressure to create lines of new and innovative products continues, as evidenced by the 92 percent of the senior executives polled by CCL who called innovation a top driver of organizational strategy. What kind of leadership supports innovation? Is that the leadership to which you aspire? Think about the following questions:

- What has been the impact of technology on you as an employee? As a leader?
- Is your role about finding the next innovation for the organization or preserving a cash cow?
- Has this trend contributed to your feeling adrift and unable to adapt to the changing environment? If so, in what way?
- Is burnout from the 24/7 access people have to you contributing to the drift you might be experiencing?
- Do you believe you can keep up with all of the technological innovations relevant to your work?

We've just discussed trends that are changing the way that organizations, leaders, and individual contributors work. What other trends could we have listed that affect you now?

WHAT DO THESE CHANGES MEAN FOR YOU AS A LEADER?

Shifts that are external and internal to organizations often demand that leaders think and behave differently from the past. Being attuned to these shifts and resulting demands keeps leaders at the forefront of what organizations need and maintains their value to the organization.

In Chapter One, we wrote about the need for leaders at all levels in organizations (what some might call collective leadership), not just at the top. Now you know why. In order to increase flexibility and speed in responding to customers, organizations need to decentralize management and provide leadership at numerous intersections across functional boundaries and at more customer touch points. As a result, all levels of the organization need shared understanding of organizational vision, strategy, and execution. Old patterns of command and control are replaced by or mixed with patterns in which who controls and who commands are in constant flux. More than ever before, leadership is as much about influence and interdependence as it is about authority. The growth of collaborations, alliances, and value chains has shifted the boundaries of effective management so that the emphasis falls on working relationships fueled by good communication. Leadership also means paying attention to organizational culture, since culture guides employees and how they interact with customers.

John McGuire and Gary Rhodes (2009) distinguish three types of organizational cultures:

- *Dependent*. Those in formal positions of authority are responsible for leadership.
- *Independent*. Leadership emerges based on technical knowledge and expertise.
- *Interdependent*. Leadership is a collective and interdependent activity.

As leaders face more complex challenges that defy easily identifiable solutions, McGuire and Rhodes argue, they need to move from dependent and independent leadership cultures to an interdependent one.

What does all of this mean for your own leader skills and perspectives? It means you have to understand the complex issues involved in coordinating systems and promoting collaboration across boundaries, and develop the means of paying attention to the interdependencies among various people and systems. Leaders must continuously respond to a variety of work routines, communication patterns, and performance standards. Harnessing collaboration becomes more important to leaders than worker supervision and managing upward. Leaders must develop the ability in themselves and their staff to discern customer needs and to be innovative, responsive, flexible, and comfortable with ambiguity and change. The days are gone when a leader can simply stay the course and manage incrementally. In organizations large and small, leaders need to reexamine and reenvision all aspects of the organization-customer interface. They must also reach out and function effectively across boundaries of time zones, geographies, gender, countries, cultures, religions, and worldviews, leading a diverse and dispersed workforce.

Take a moment here to review the contextual challenges your organization faces and the impact they have on your own leadership and the leadership of your colleagues. It's important to consider both the potential benefits of these changes (for example, opportunities to be involved in leadership roles even when you don't have the formal title, or chances to work on issues that make important differences in the lives of others) and their costs. Unknown costs may push you into drift, making you temporarily unable to take action. Think about what you have seen going on around you, and consider the implications for how you lead, how you can be even more effective as a leader, and how you might work your way out of drift:

- How do these contextual challenges manifest themselves in your organization and industry?
- What implications have the changes had for leaders in your organization?
- Do you see different kinds of leaders evolving now than in the past?
- How has the changing nature of leadership affected you? What new skill sets or perspectives do you need to develop in order to be effective in the years to come?
- What opportunities for leadership are presented to you that a decade ago may not have been possible?
- How have these changes helped or challenged you recently as a leader?
- How have any of these trends or changing skills contributed to drift in your work?

- How have other individuals failed because they didn't adapt to the changing times?
- What do you want to do differently as a result of gaining insight into your current context?

CHANGING PERSPECTIVES
ON LEADERSHIP

As organizations have become more complex and the problems that leaders face more challenging, definitions of successful leadership have also expanded. Let's look at how views or perspectives on leadership have evolved over the years, beginning with the idea that leaders aren't necessarily identified by title or job description and that current diverse and rapidly changing contexts mean that new and different leaders can emerge at any time. Expanding your perspectives on leadership can be both motivating and overwhelming. Your challenge is to understand the impact that contemporary perspectives have on your own views and images of leaders and leadership. You will also want to think about the compatibility of your views with those of others, and how these may contribute to feelings of drift or your own perceptions of choice. Think too about what view you wish to instill in others.

Nine Common Perspectives on Leadership
The nine common perspectives on leadership that follow blend fact and fiction, stories and experience—the received, unquestioned beliefs of a particular culture. Each perspective carries its own implications, though people can easily hold several of them simultaneously. Some perspectives deal with who becomes a leader and how, and others with how a leader should lead. As you read them, think about how they might affect your sense of yourself as a leader and the ways you interpret that role. Also think about the contexts in which you lead and which of these perspectives is appropriate—or not. Keep in mind that there is no single right perspective; one size does not fit all.

Leaders Are Born

This fixed mind-set holds that some people are born with leadership talent and others are not. In other words, only certain people can learn to lead effectively; they're naturals. If you were born with it, you are destined to lead. If you were not, you will never lead.

Leadership Can Be Learned

In this view, you can study leadership carefully, practice what you study, and become a more effective leader, no matter how good you are now. This is the opposite of the genetic "leaders are born" view. Research in the social and neurosciences increasingly suggests that human characteristics we once thought of as permanent (like IQ, personality, and some cognitive skills) are actually malleable through learning.

Leaders Are Heroes

From this perspective, the only good leaders are those who perform risky, courageous, wise, and benevolent feats that are beyond the rest of us. These heroes, always handsome or beautiful, are extroverted and charismatic, and they command attention whenever they walk into a room. Think about the characters portrayed by John Wayne, Clint Eastwood, Denzel Washington, Angelina Jolie, and Meryl Streep. Some are leaders with the uncanny ability to get the rest of us out of trouble. Or think of real-life recent heroes such as Erin Brockovich (in the toxic wastewater case against Pacific Gas and Electric) or executive Sherron Watkins, who called out Enron's massive fraud.

Leaders Are at the Top

This is the view that leadership happens only at or close to the top of an organization. In command-and-control environments, your role is to simply follow orders unless you occupy a top position. If you're not on the senior leadership team, you are perceived as having little leadership to offer. Members of management hold the cards, for better or worse.

Leaders Are Called to Serve

When it's your time to lead, you'll be asked. When asked, you should accept and be grateful. After all, not everyone is asked. Social scripts create expectations about who is likely to be asked to lead and, when asked, how a leader should behave given the context in which he or she functions. We often internalize such scripts from powerful influences from early family life and our surrounding cultures; although sometimes difficult to identify, their effects are profound.

Leaders Are Defined by Position

If you're in the job and have the title, you're the leader. This notion is traditional in bureaucracies and highly structured organizations, and it carries some validity even in less hierarchical systems. If your title says "director of" or "head of," your leadership abilities and effectiveness are assumed unassailable. You have power, authority, and possibly a corner office.

Leaders Depend on and Are Created by Others

Some leaders view the deep involvement of other people in setting direction and making decisions as the cornerstone of a leader's success. In this view, the leader's goal is to unleash the talents of others. The view focuses on the collective and interdependent processes we discussed earlier in connection with transformational leadership. As Lao Tzu is quoted as saying, "A leader is best when people barely know he exists, when his work is done, his aim fulfilled, they will say: we did it ourselves."

Leadership Is Temporary

Organizations lacking a pipeline of leadership talent are often forced to select a sometimes reluctant leader with an "interim" title or status, to fulfill a leadership function. Individuals often take on such roles because they are persuaded to do so or are strongly committed to the organization. Some grow into their leadership role and by mutual agreement become officially more permanent. Others accept the assignment for a limited time while the organization selects a more permanent leader.

Leaders Are Servants

A call to lead out of a desire to serve others can be quite compelling to some people. It involves a deeply felt sense of mission, private purpose, inevitability, or legacy. The call may be so powerful that the person feels practically unable to turn down a leadership opportunity. A calling isn't always rational, but it's personally passionate. The servant leader doesn't leave it to others to judge whether his or her desire to serve others is valid or appropriate. Equally compelling might be the absence of that inner voice.

What Can Be Gained from Exploring?

Each of these views is worth exploring and can lead you to unexpected places. When a particular view doesn't match the organizational context, for example, questions can arise as to whether a leader is the right fit for the organization: Can this person be successful in this role or this environment? When the view is reinforced and rewarded, value and excitement can be realized.

Some organizations may operate as a strict hierarchy, despite signals of a more equally competitive environment or the advances in communication technology. Other organizations reward individuals for following a social script. Some organizations may intentionally change the kind of leadership perspectives that it rewards, and so confusion may run rampant. You may need to do some digging to understand which view or set of views predominates in your organization. History, culture, and existing leadership will have a great influence here.

Consider this story about a servant leader whose own questions of fit led him to seek other choices.

For many years, Paul wished he were helping others see their potential as individuals and as members of a tightly knit community. An early career in sales had been disappointing: it made a living and the products were honest, but they didn't come close to touching lives.

Paul left sales for the seminary and became a minister, but ministry didn't work for him either. To him it seemed too parochial and ritualistic. Next, he accepted an offer from a nonprofit organization that needed a manager to run a unit that provided development experiences for people across the country. Paul did well at this work. His staff liked him, and his counseling skills were useful. For a while, the world seemed fine. Then Paul found that the organization's growth meant that his leadership role was becoming more about managing than serving. So at a time of peak effectiveness in his organizational career, he stepped away from running a department and became an individual contributor within the organization. Paul found he could promote his deeply held values more explicitly when he worked side by side with others and could serve as a sounding board and mentor.

For now, at least, the world seems fine to Paul. He's found a comfortable and effective way to be what he wants to be. We believe that in his new role as an individual contributor, he will have ample opportunities to be a leader, even if his span of control is narrower than it was previously and his budget lower.

The Value of Knowing Your Views

The views of leadership we've described aren't mutually exclusive, and your own are no doubt a blend of many ideas, experiences, worldviews, and theories. Views of leadership are informed by success, trial and error, input from others (such as coaches, friends, family, and coworkers), and observing the good and bad practices of leaders. You're much better off if you're aware of your own views and how you and others might be affected by them.

If you pay attention to your own changing views and the views of others, you can develop yourself to take better advantage of opportunities and overcome inevitable obstacles that can cause you to drift into inaction. Certain choices about leading may seem desirable and make more sense to you than others do. It's important to maintain broad attention and see how these philosophies or views of leadership may be relevant to your work today.

The difference between managers who are comfortable as leaders and those who aren't is that the former can articulate the views and images of leadership that guide them through thick and thin and that integrate career, family, and community. That awareness helps them recognize how well they match the leadership roles their organizations envision, and they make work and career decisions accordingly.

To help you integrate the views of leadership in your environment and in yourself, we encourage you to develop a flexible but sustaining personal view of leadership. How you think about leadership should be based on what you want to accomplish in life. Why are you leading? Your views of leadership aren't cast in stone. At each stage of your life and career, you will need to question and rebuild your views based on new learning and new experiences. The more comprehensive your view and the more frequently you reflect on it, the better it will serve you as an integrating tool.

Some of the following questions may sound simple, and you may already have addressed them. But if you haven't taken the time to stop and reflect on your answers in some while or have never considered the power of such questions to illuminate your decision to serve as a leader, we encourage you to do so now:

- How will being a leader help you create the impact you desire?
- Which views about leadership (from those previously described or those you have experienced elsewhere) resonate with you? Why?
- Which view or views about leadership are disagreeable to you? Why?
- How conscious are you of your leadership views? How do they play out in your behavior?
- What views of leadership have been preferred in organizations in which you have worked?
- How closely matched are your views and those of your organization, or how closely matched are your views and the views of people you lead?
- What changes in your view might make you a more effective leader in the contexts in which you now lead?

By now, you recognize the amount of complexity flowing from continuous change in organizations as well as from expanding views of leadership. This complexity is not without its consequences or costs, which is where our discussion now turns.

INCREASING DEMANDS ON LEADERS

More leaders than ever before question whether they were right to have chosen the leadership path. Many ask: Is being a leader worth the effort and sacrifice? For example, a survey by Adecco Group North America found that 61 percent of employees would decline to take their manager's position with its greater pressures (Winter, 2009).

In the letter excerpted below, a senior leader who attended a CCL program articulates how he needs to better allocate his time across work and nonwork activities so that the cost-benefit ratio of leading is more favorable to his overall well-being. This is the first of several excerpted letters that we include in this book . These letters were written by executives to themselves as part of a classroom-based goal-setting activity (they are all italicized to help you find them easily):

Dear—

It is time for you to reflect on your life and decide how you will spend the next half of it.

It's time to decide to be a happier person by taking more time for yourself, taking family trips to the coast or the mountains. Travel to places you have never been and return to those that you love. Play your guitar more, write songs that have been waiting to come out. Describe the world as only you can see it. Visit those that are special to you and tell them so. Play music and share it with others.

Continue your education, not for some fancy degree, but for the experience and for the sake of learning something new.

Follow your passion, not your pension.

Be more loving and affectionate to those you love most, your family—

Most of all, love yourself. Care less about others' opinions of you and more about your heart. Be kind to yourself. Relax and enjoy the ride.

It's important to understand the demands inherent in many leadership positions. Use all of the information at your disposal to determine what those demands are in your case. The managers we spoke to while writing this book never hesitated over questions about costs, sacrifices, and difficulties. They told us about high stress levels, irritability, dealing with problem performers, or having to lay off employees. Some bemoaned a loss of freedom. These costs were obviously painful, though, as one said, "If you assume the mantle, you've got to pay the price." Understanding these demands helps you develop strategies to offset them, ignore them, neutralize them, or seek a different role where the costs are lower.

Here are the types of costs that were frequently mentioned. Of course, what is a cost to one leader may be some kind of reward for another.

Visibility

You're in the fishbowl, and all eyes are on you: "Who's she spending time with?" "Who's he including in his meetings?" "Why is she having lunch with him?" "Did you hear what he did to her?" "Take a look at what she's wearing today." "He's in a bad mood—must be fighting with his wife again." As one executive said, "Just walking out in my work area (there are ninety folks in my operation), I know they watch me all the time.... It's like walking a tightrope."

Public Duties

The higher you rise in an organization, the more you appear as its brand and spokesperson, and so the more you take on public relations responsibilities. You give speeches and make introductions for other speakers. Your attendance is required at community dinners, cocktail parties, receptions, fundraising activities, and so forth. You greet and entertain visiting dignitaries. These are important tasks. Shirk them at your peril.

Separation

The leader is no longer one of the gang. The former peer group is gone, and the new one sometimes is made up of people who are competitors for other choice spots. It's important for leaders to maintain some personal distance from their colleagues. Relationships that become too close can lead to faulty decisions or considerable pain when, say, reducing staff. It's not that leaders must be isolated socially; rather, they often lose long-lasting, genuinely comfortable relationships that are hard to replace. They miss the few people with whom they can openly talk.

Caretaking and Emotional Strain

Leaders are responsible for those they lead and are often expected to take care of others. Care ranges from helping others improve in their roles, to setting performance expectations, to listening to personal disappointments. These activities are important and require time and energy. On many managers, responsibility for direct reports weighs heavily. One executive we spoke with observed, "You have a significant measure of control over people's lives. You know—promotions and demotions and firings. You have to be willing to understand that and make judgments and do it extremely carefully. In a way, you're really fulfilling a trust that some organization is putting on you."

Trust is the foundation on which relationships are built and in the collaborative climate within which current organizations operate relationships are how work gets done. Therefore, leaders feel tremendous responsibility for not violating any trust as they navigate to meet organizational and individual needs.

Stamina

Leadership requires energy, stamina, and the ability to impart to others. It often brings with it long hours, long meetings, loads of e-mail, and little time for family and recreation. Don't mention the travel, with its stuffy waiting rooms, bad food, cramped seats, and delayed flights. Exhaustion hovers, and you have to take care of yourself. CCL research indicates a strong correlation between health and leadership effectiveness. Leaders with better health status (as measured by physiological factors such as blood lipid and blood glucose levels and body-mass index ratings) were more likely to be seen by peers, direct reports, and bosses as effective leaders than were their less healthy counterparts.

Job Insecurity

Leadership roles are not secure. Most senior executives in public and private organizations rate job security lower than anything else about their organizations. Senior leaders are judged on the basis of the success of the whole enterprise, which results from many influences beyond their control. Merit is defined and rewarded more selectively for leadership than for professional roles. And leaders can't discount politics or career dynamics. Someone else may really want your spot, or just may not want you in it anymore. In cases of mergers and acquisitions, leaders can find that they are redundant.

Less Freedom of Expression

The higher you climb in an organization, the greater the need is to tightly regulate your words and expression of feelings. People will weigh your speech more heavily than the speech of those below you. You can't think aloud because people may interpret your musings as directives. You may want to relax, joke around, and be one of the gang, but even in relaxed situations, people are keenly aware of what you say and how you behave. You must always be aware of your image.

Infrequent Relief and Its Strain on Your Family

You must keep an eye on the bigger picture (people expect you to see around corners and beyond the horizon) while focusing attention on current priorities. You must also be able to determine which small brush fire might turn wild. You receive few easy breaks and may take work home every night just to stay on top of your priorities. Even on weekends or on vacations, you're probably mulling over work issues. Your name is first on the emergency call list, and you are copied daily on, say, a hundred or more consequential e-mails. One bank executive told us, "I think my family has probably paid more than it should. I have a tendency to be a workaholic, and so if anything has suffered, it's been my personal life. I have this psychological thing, you know—as long as it's light out, I can work. When the sun goes down, I go home." Another executive reported, "The biggest cost is actually to the self, because you're forced into limited time for self and family, and so the self goes far down on the list. Family takes a hit, and you feel bad about the family. So you try to take more and more out of the self portion to prop up the family."

Infrequent Honest Feedback

When you need honest appraisal the most, you are less likely to find it. The higher your rise in an organization, the less useful the feedback you receive is. Everyone else seems to have some personal bias or agenda; information is plentiful, but the truth is elusive. People are prone to tell you what they think you want to hear rather than what you need to hear. Good leaders sometimes identify truth tellers in the organization to mitigate this problem, but such people aren't easy to find because there are often consequences to being the truth teller (for example, others in the organization may view truth tellers as simply trying to advance their status with the boss).

These costs we've discussed don't comprise an exhaustive list. You may have other costs that are specific to your leadership scenario. Do those costs contribute to your leadership drift? Do they push you into action? Think about and document the costs you experience.

Of course, there are also rewards, though these can also lead to drift. Sometimes you can be so attached to a reward that you stay in a role too long. We discuss benefits and rewards further in Chapter Six. There you will have the opportunity to weigh the costs and benefits of your current and future leadership choices.

CONCLUSION

In this chapter, we described changes in organizations and the resulting expectations placed on leaders, and the fact that more than ever before, leaders wonder if the cost is worth the rewards. Our discussion surveyed shifting perspectives and views about leadership today that can complicate your choice to lead.

Reflect on the following final questions to better understand your leadership context:

- What are the most important organizational factors that have an impact on you?
- Have changes in the context pushed you into a state of drift?
- What are the current leadership demands on you that provide motivation or frustration, or both?
- Have you clarified your own views on leadership and how they are compatible with others in the organization?
- What are you experiencing as the costs of leading right now, and do you need to reduce the costs to be a more effective leader?
- What insights about drift in your own leadership scenario have you gained from this chapter?

In Chapter Three, we look at leadership vision and how it can clarify your actions and choices and lead you out of drift.

CHAPTER THREE

YOUR LEADERSHIP VISION

In Chapter Two we discussed some of the organizational factors influencing leadership, as well as common perspectives and views of it. Whether those views come from your surrounding culture, your organization, or some other source, they can affect the way you see yourself as a leader and your expectations of what leaders do. In this chapter, we examine vision, a key part of discovering the leader in you. Indeed, if you cannot articulate a clear and compelling vision for leadership, your risk of drift is higher, and you may be less able to escape it. Think about it: How can you effectively chart a course out of drift if you don't have a clear view (that is, a vision) of where you want to go?

A leadership vision is foundational to your views of leadership and your long-term success as a leader. Your vision for leadership goes beyond simple expectations and perspectives about the role of a leader. It captures and describes the desired future that you see for yourself and your team, organization, or community. A vision for leadership is different from an organizational mission (which spells out the reason for an entity to exist) and from organizational goals (which articulate specific outcomes). Your leadership vision is an expression of what you want to create, do, or accomplish when you are in a leader role. It describes your philosophy about leadership and your purpose in choosing to be a leader, and it serves as an important guidepost for the core behaviors you enact as a leader.

CONSCIOUS PERSONAL AND LEADERSHIP VISIONS

A leadership vision is not the same as your personal vision. Rather, it is a component of your personal vision; it can help you accomplish the larger vision for your life, which also encompasses other life roles, family desires, where you want to retire, and so on.

Similarly, a leadership vision isn't a specific organizational vision or the future state desired by leaders of a particular organization. Your leadership vision is that which you personally want to accomplish with your leadership. For example, if, like Michael J. Fox, finding a cure for Parkinson's disease were your leadership vision, then you could find many ways to demonstrate your leadership, such as starting a foundation to raise money to support research, going to medical school to learn more about the disease and then treating it, or publishing a newsletter to raise public awareness about the disease.

Conveying a compelling leadership vision is foundational to being an effective leader. CCL research with senior leaders reveals that leaders who are able to articulate a clear and compelling vision for their organization are rated by bosses and peers as more effective leaders.

As a child, you may have "known" that you would someday become an astronaut, a professional athlete, a teacher, or a doctor. As you grew and advanced through school, you might have expressed what you "knew" about yourself by seeking out other young people who shared your interests. Later you began to see yourself in adult roles, such as a family and community member and as a contributor to the organization where you work. Through these stages, you may have woven a vision for leadership into your life. You might not have spelled out that vision in a personal creed or blogged to the world, but it was there.

We've found that leaders at all levels often have at least a rudimentary vision of leadership under the surface. True, some haven't been particularly thoughtful about their lives or reflected on their experiences to imagine what's to come. As a reader of this book, you're unlikely to be one of them. But your leadership vision may still lie below the level of awareness, and thus it's not available to regularly draw on in your role as a leader. Unarticulated, it leaves too much to chance and leaves you vulnerable to drift, it leaves you less than fully engaged, and it leaves you passive and opportunistic in your work.

Without question, who you are as a person and what you want to accomplish in your life (your legacy) influences your vision for leadership. It is this conscious connection between your personal vision and the leadership vision that creates congruency of direction. Consider how one senior executive with whom we worked thought about his legacy (including what he did as a leader) in strongly personal terms:

> *Dear—*
>
> *CCL confirmed to you that you're a leader—embrace that and have fun with it. Don't be so hard on yourself—got it. When you're eulogized, people will remember you as a good man who left a legacy of a happy marriage, kids who grew to be productive adults, and a leader who inspired others and was fun to be around. Lastly, you'll be remembered for the people you helped pull up. Life is like a baseball game, and you were lucky enough to have been born on 2nd base. Look around for people having trouble getting into the stadium and give them a hand. Now call your parents.*

Think about how having a similarly vivid picture of your legacy might influence your vision for leadership. What do you want your legacy to be? How is your leadership a part of this legacy?

Personal vision and leadership vision can intersect powerfully. Colleagues at CCL brought back this story from a recent trip to India where they had visited with leaders of Pantaloons, one of India's fast-growing retail companies. At the time, Pantaloons was keenly focused on developing the skills of its leaders and frontline workers. Most of them earn low salaries and come from the lowest socioeconomic strata of Indian society. A member of the Pantaloons training arm had begun a leader development program based on a personal insight he gained from the streets of Mumbai as he watched beggars work the traffic intersections. Sympathetically, he noticed that some beggars were more effective in obtaining charity than others. "What is the difference?" he wondered. Careful observation suggested that the more effective beggars displayed a greater sense of self-confidence and self-worth. If he was right, these personal characteristics, which could be nurtured, taught, and developed, could be applied to those who worked at Pantaloons. From that insight, he implemented a visionary, innovative developmental program that ultimately strengthened employee engagement and subsequent organizational performance. His story shows how an individual with a higher purpose can connect his leadership vision to the needs of a group (not the beggars themselves, but others in lower socioeconomic brackets than his) and the needs of a growing business. It shows how a leadership commitment to helping the less fortunate was blended into an innovative hiring and employee development initiative.

Or consider Muhammad Yunus, founder of Grameen Bank. In 1974, Yunus was an economics professor in Bangladesh; at the time, Bangladesh was experiencing yet another famine. The problem was so large that he questioned whether he could help in any meaningful way. One day Yunus visited a village near the university at which he was teaching to learn more about what he could do to help the villagers cope with hunger. He discovered that the forty-two women in the village wanted a total of twenty-seven dollars to start small businesses so that they could take care of their families in a more sustainable way. After extensive efforts to persuade banks to loan the women money, Yunus took twenty-seven dollars out of his own wallet and funded the women to establish microenterprises. This small investment had astounding and unexpected ripple effects. Indeed, it was the impetus for what eventually led to global microfinance movement.

As of this writing, Grameen Bank had made over $10 billion in loans to over 7 million borrowers, almost all women. The loan recovery rate is over 98 percent, which is better than institutions that lend to higher-income clients. With twenty-four hundred branches, Grameen Bank provides services in many tens of thousands of villages. All of this was started by an economics professor who felt helpless in fighting hunger and poverty and so simply loaned twenty-seven dollars from his own pocket. This work has had such a powerful impact that Yunus and Grameen Bank were awarded the 2006 Nobel Peace Prize. The global innovation of microfinance that Yunus and a few dozen poor women in a single village set in motion provides a powerful example of how a compelling, personally derived leadership vision can achieve monumental change that drives business outcomes and improves the daily lives of customers.

DISCOVERING OR CLARIFYING YOUR LEADERSHIP VISION

Almost daily, we interact with leaders who struggle to find and articulate a meaningful vision for their work as leaders. Tackling this issue head-on is not easy. It requires deeply exploring what motivates you to get up in the morning and drives your attention and energy throughout the day.

As we said earlier, a leadership vision is an expression of what you want to create, do, or accomplish as a leader. To serve as a useful guide, your vision should do three things:

1. It should incorporate your dreams and passions—the things that motivate and excite you about leading.
2. It should be authentic and anchored in who you are as a person. It must reflect your values about leadership.
3. It should continue to evolve. A leadership vision is not static, like a photograph. Rather, it is like daily frames in a slow-motion film. It reflects where you are in your own evolution and where you think you are heading in your own life journey.

Not many leaders spend time thinking about their leadership vision. One told us (typically), "I think mainly in terms of management. I was thinking more in terms of job and job description than I was in terms of leadership and what I had to do." However, one technical manager we met at a chemical company had given it quite a bit of thought: "Leadership is all about being able to formulate a vision, deciding that you want to go somewhere, that there is value in getting there, and then being able to describe that vision, to sell that vision. The word *lead* comes in when you bring people along with you to attain it."

Having a leadership vision is not just for those at the top. Sure, it is often easier to pursue your own leadership vision and what you want to accomplish as a leader when you are at the helm, but a clear leadership vision can still empower a middle manager or frontline supervisor. Perhaps your leadership vision is to help fix what is broken, saving money and time. If so, it will matter in many contexts: mending the broken spirits of people who were led by an ineffective leader, rejuvenating an old product line in decline, or restoring a brand that was damaged by recall, for example.

STRATEGIES FOR DISCOVERING A LEADERSHIP VISION

Developing your own leadership vision is difficult; simply adopting someone else's vision won't work. Clarifying your vision is an ongoing journey involving a process of exploring likely places for elements you can combine to form a conscious, meaningful, and integrated picture. You discover your vision by honestly looking at yourself and your role as a leader in an organization or community.

The rest of this chapter suggests strategies to help you discover or clarify your leadership vision and make it more visible to yourself and others. Whether you have never thought of having a leadership vision and are starting from scratch, or you have one but it needs more definition, depth, or expansion, the following strategies will take you through various reflective processes to assist you in your work. If you gravitate to some of the strategies more than others and don't feel a need for all of them, simply use the ones that help you the most in clarifying your leadership vision. Here they are, in short:

- Tell your own story.
- Reflect on your daydreams.

- Look for trends and patterns.
- Incorporate lessons from role models.
- Assess your perspectives on power and conflict.
- Make use of your creative involvement.
- Follow your intuition.
- Look beyond yourself.

Tell Your Own Story

There's a book in you: the one you're writing about your own life. Narrative is innate to human growth, and personal vision often springs from myth or one's imagination. The same can happen for a leadership vision. When people discover, create, invent, build businesses, raise families, compose symphonies, or fly to the moon, they do it to fulfill a story that they've been telling themselves and others. Think about your own story and how it is part of your leadership journey:

> If we wish to know about a man we ask, "What is his story—his real, inmost story?" For each of us is a biography, . . . a singular narrative which is constructed continually, unconsciously, by, through, and in us—through our perceptions, our feelings, our thoughts, our notions. Biologically, physiologically, we are not so different from each other; historically, as narratives, we are each of us unique [Sacks, 1970, pp. 110–111].

The richer and more compelling you can make the story of yourself as a leader, the stronger your leadership vision will be. People tell and retell their stories until they get them right. Your own story is connected to those you inherited from others. This story from one of the leaders we know gives a sense of that continuity:

> I had an older brother that I really looked up to, nine years older than me. I was in about fourth grade when he got killed in Vietnam. At that time, my mother told me that I had to be the head of the household. I think that had a profound effect on me. That was a catalyst. I went from being a child to being responsible from that day forward.

I've been in leadership types of positions ever since I was in high school. In high school, it started out with sports. Then I got real serious about politics in high school, and I got involved in some political groups in the sixties. [Now] I'm involved in a number of different nonprofit organizations . . . and I have leadership roles in every one of them.

Some stories take generations to tell and to complete. Others are picked up as inspirational waypoints, and the people they're associated with are regarded as pioneers. Some people relish the idea of rewriting their stories over and over again. But even if you don't, we're sure that you've revised and improvised your story over the years, and we are also sure that the basic theme of your story shows continuity over time. Within that push and pull of change and continuity, your vision of yourself as a leader emerges. Take a moment to think about your story and its recurring themes, especially as they relate to your roles as a leader. Think about your life as a series of headlines in a newspaper:

- What events have inspired your passion?
- What stories would you tell about making a difference as a leader?
- What stories would your colleagues tell about you as a leader?
- What actions have reflected your values or have made an enduring impression on you?
- What would you want a journalist to write about your vision as a leader?

Reflect on Your Daydreams

Everybody daydreams—sometimes in quiet moments, sometimes as we're drifting off to sleep, and sometimes when we're engaged in physical activity like walking or running. Although most leaders will rarely admit it publicly, we're sure that many occasionally daydream in a boring meeting.

Daydreams can be important sources of insight, a window into something deeper than they seem, connecting present realities to some desired future state. Indeed, they may even reflect your aspirations as a person and a leader and sketch a bridge to their fulfillment. As Henry David Thoreau noted, "If one advances confidently in the direction of his dreams, and endeavors to live the life which he has imagined, he will meet with a success unexpected in common hours." We suggest the content of your daydreams can help you articulate a leadership vision.

When you catch yourself daydreaming, make a few notes, and reflect on how they would connect to your vision for leadership. Do you see any obvious connections? Can you make some not-so-obvious connections between your leadership vision and the daydream's seemingly random thoughts? A daydream may reveal an image of yourself as a leader—the kind of successes you're having, how you see yourself as a winner or hero, the kinds of situations you're in, things that bother or worry you, and what you do to contribute to the success of a team. Daydreams can inform how we see ourselves and how we want to be seen by others—what you might call *self-image*. By noticing when and where you perceive a positive self-image, you can get a glimpse of the vision you are trying to project or a picture of where you're trying to go in your life as a leader.

As you reflect on your daydreams as a mirror into your leadership vision, it is important to connect them to actions. As *Harry Potter* author J. K. Rowling says, "It does not do to dwell on dreams and forget to live" (1998, p. 214). With perceptive humor, Mitch Hedberg (2003) says, "I'm sick of following my dreams. I'm just going to ask them where they're going and hook up with them later." His comment harkens back to our discussion in Chapter One about drifting into leadership versus making a conscious, active choice to pursue it.

Thomas Jefferson imagined a set of principles about how free people should live in relationship to their government, and then he enacted those principles in a lifetime of founding, expanding, and leading a vast country; creating a university; and contributing mightily to the philosophy that undergirds the United States to this day. When Dr. Martin Luther King Jr. said, "I have a dream," to a crowd in front of the Lincoln Memorial in 1963, his words and deeds helped crystallize a nonviolent civil rights movement. Christopher Reeve (1999), the actor-turned-advocate for biomedical research and spinal injury patients said, "So many of our dreams at first seem impossible, then they seem improbable, and then, when we summon the will, they soon become inevitable" (p. 300).

Dreams of smaller scope can be equally inspiring, and they don't have to be entirely original. King borrowed from Gandhi, and Jefferson borrowed from the philosophers of the European Enlightenment. As the song in the Broadway musical *Finian's Rainbow* (Harburg and Saidy, 1947) put it, people will "follow the fellow who follows the dream."

Take a moment now to jot down what you've been daydreaming about lately, and remind yourself for the next few days to remember what you were daydreaming about and how that might help you develop a leadership vision:

- Are there common themes in your daydreams that reflect on your vision or aspirations as a leader?
- As you think about your past successes and failures as a leader, are there connections you can make between these past experiences and your current daydreams?
- If you could write your own daydream of yourself exhibiting exceptional leadership skills, how would it go?
- If your leadership scenario indicates you feel stuck, bored, pressured, or similarly unhappy, what solutions are you pondering in your daydreams?
- If money were no object, where would you work? What cause or passion would you pursue?

Look for Trends and Patterns

Another way to bring your leadership vision to light is to look for patterns in events you have experienced, behaviors you have engaged in, attitudes that you hold. We're not suggesting that you synthesize a complex map—only to look for repeating or similar themes when you play back part of the tape of your life experiences. Patterns are not always neatly labeled, and they may be more obvious to people around you than they are to you. So feel free to seek the guidance of family members or close friends and colleagues as you document key life trends and patterns.

Start by noticing broad patterns. In the past, what things have you repeatedly paid attention to, gravitated toward, or chosen to do in your work and personal life? For example, one leader we know had chosen as a teenager to attend an all-girls' high school and found there that girls naturally stepped into leadership roles when they were not competing against boys. This experience was the start of her interest in women and leadership, and her later choices throughout her life reinforced the early pattern. Look at your experiences and the passions that hold you, the books you choose to read, the television shows you watch, the quotes or stories that resonate with you. As you think about these early experiences and choices, do you see any connections to your leadership work?

Next, note the important events that you have experienced during the past year or two—especially key projects, activities, and relationships at work. What trends and patterns might you notice in how you spend your time, and what kinds of work attract you?

After you've reviewed some of the broader themes in your experiences, you can more closely examine your behaviors and the roles you play in groups. There are two kinds of lessons for you to gather at this stage. One has to do with how eagerly you engage directly in leadership roles and what kinds of leadership roles you embrace; the other has to do with where you typically try to lead the groups you are in, from whatever roles you play.

Consider the following questions:

- When did you have success, and when did you have setbacks? What were some contributing factors?
- When were you happiest?
- Which situations did you find easy or hard to deal with?
- What kinds of projects or teams are you asked to join?
- Which of those really interested you? Which do you avoid?

- A number of factors could be making certain activities successful, enjoyable, easy, and attractive for you. What's the underlying theme in these situations?
- What do they have in common that produces the positive experience?

Incorporate Lessons from Role Models

When we ask people about their role models, we're also asking them about their own aspirations. A person who names Bernie Madoff as a role model has a very different vision from one who names Nelson Mandela. Role models can be real or fictional, famous or private, public figures or personal acquaintants. The important feature of a role model is that you have thought about that person's image and found something attractive in it. That's the element you want to examine for clues to your leadership vision.

This isn't about picking a hero. Ask yourself a series of questions about why such a person interests you so much:

- Do you name Bill Gates because he is bright, because he is among the richest persons in the world, or because of his vast philanthropic activities?
- Do you admire Nelson Mandela because he overcame adversity, because he became a national savior, or because of the way he performed in office?
- Is Muhammad Yunus your role model because he won the Nobel Peace Prize in 2006 for developing the microfinance model or because he commands the attention of world leaders?
- Is one of the reasons you admire your Aunt Charlene that she travels all over the world and doesn't ask anyone's permission to do anything?

One executive told us what he learned from one role-model boss in his career, the chief financial officer at *Esquire* magazine:

> He would never let anybody go unless he was satisfied that he had done everything that he could to make that person work out in

the position. He was essentially telling me that I needed to take as much responsibility as the other person and do everything that I could to make a situation work. That's a large, transcending statement. People look for the easy way out, but there has to be a lot of personal ownership in leadership.

Make a short list of the role models you've followed in life. For each of them, ask yourself the following questions:

- Why is this person a role model for you?
- How are this person's admirable characteristics similar to and dissimilar from yours?
- In what ways did this person exhibit leadership?
- What is this person's leadership vision? How was it communicated and put into practice? What made it compelling to others?

Assess Your Perspectives on Power and Conflict
Leadership entails using power on occasion. In fact, leadership is about the power to make things happen. Because power has many negative connotations, people often talk about it as influence, impact, or effectiveness. But power itself is neutral. It is the outcomes of using one's power, and whether those outcomes are perceived as good or bad, that determine how effectively power has been used. As Abraham Lincoln noted, "Nearly all men can stand adversity, but if you want to test a man's character, give him power."

How do you feel about having and using power? Where is power in your leadership vision? What part does it play? How does your power affect your ability to relate to other people?

With power comes conflict—no question about that. Like power, conflict is an inevitable part of life as a leader. Across many studies conducted at CCL on the topic of executive derailment, the ability to handle conflict effectively is a key factor that differentiates leaders who don't derail from those who do.

Conflict is inevitable when two people in positions of power or of leadership don't agree. If you embrace conflict as a common element of work life, it can be highly informative and a stimulus for bringing transparency to core issues such as vision and values. Conflict can draw out what you and others hold valuable and are willing to advocate for, defend, and protect. If you understand the effect that values have on how people respond to different situations, then you can better understand the root causes of a conflict. And in understanding root causes, you will also gain insight into the way values affect your vision for leadership.

For some people, leveraging power and managing conflict in pursuit of a leadership vision can be an anxious endeavor. Some never planned to take power, so when conflict arises, as it will in any opportunity to lead, they fall back on old scripts about the importance of modesty, fairness, and not stepping on toes in pursuit of control and influence. This sort of interference isn't easy to sort out, but it's worth your time to try if you find yourself uneasy with power and conflict. If you can view your interactions with others as an opportunity to share and leverage power for a higher purpose, your effectiveness as a leader and the effectiveness of your group are likely to increase.

You might encounter power and conflict in a variety of situations. For example, have you ever been in a situation in which you thought, "Enough is enough!" and insisted on breaking with the status quo? Have you ever lost a leadership position because you believed that the direction that was being taken was wrong? Have you found yourself in a prolonged debate about the merits of a decision or strategy? Have you told someone in a senior position that doing it your way wasn't just better but a lot better, or maybe even the only way to succeed? Consider these questions on power and conflict:

- How does power fit into your conceptions of yourself and your vision for leadership? What do you like and dislike about power?
- How have you used power effectively and ineffectively?
- When you admire others' use of power, what do you admire about them, and what does that convey to you about their leadership vision?
- What does misuse of power look like?

- How do you feel and act when you don't have power?
- What ideas or goals have you fought for in recent years?
- What have you gone to the mat about? What does that say about your values and your vision for leadership?
- How well do you handle conflict?
- In various conflicts you have with others, is there a theme or pattern in the content of the disagreement?
- Do you tend to get in conflict with a particular group of people?
- How does conflict affect your vision about how you want to lead?

Make Note of Your Creative Involvement

Where you expend your creative energies tells you a lot about your passions and interests and can inform your leadership vision. With respect to the relationship between creativity and vision, creativity is like a fingerprint. It can be what makes your vision for leadership unique. Part of discovering your leadership vision is noticing how you use your creative capabilities. Perhaps you love coming up with new product ideas or improving existing systems. Perhaps you love the power of the written word, and you spend extra hours writing. Perhaps you love helping people solve problems and can easily spend hours listening and thinking about their problems rather than attending to your own.

A leader's creativity can show up in connecting existing ideas that others have not previously connected. It can show up in metaphors and analogies that reinterpret old problems or in some entirely new approach. No matter what form it takes, being creative doesn't happen by chance or without expenditure of desire and effort. People who are perceived as creative will tell you that it takes preparation and hard work and can be pursued in deliberate ways. Central to it are a heightened form of focus and energy and a deep involvement with whatever you're doing.

If you have an area in your life that you consider creative (maybe you play a musical instrument, paint, write, engage in outdoor adventures, or play sports), explore what that activity says about your vision for leadership. You may find that your creative outlets tell you quite a bit about your passion, desires, and energy regarding leadership. Ask yourself the following questions:

- When do you feel most creative as a leader, and when do you feel most at ease or in the groove?
- When are you so absorbed you lose track of time? Does this ever happen when you are leading? Whether it happens or not, what does that convey to you about your vision for leadership?
- When is leadership creative? When it's not, why is that?
- Does your organization encourage your creativity? If not, is this why you feel a sense of drift?
- How do you as a leader encourage the expression of creativity among others, and what might you be doing that thwarts it?
- How do you use your creativity outside your job or leadership role? If there is a gap between your creative level at work and your creative level outside work, what do you attribute that to?

Follow Your Intuition

While we believe that developing a leadership vision requires deliberate thought and collection and analysis of data, we also believe that intuition is a source of insight into developing a vision for leadership. Why? Because leaders often lack the data they would like to have to make a decision or articulate a vision. In such moments, tapping into your intuition can help you move from analysis to action. Intuition requires:

- Bringing both creative and analytical approaches to an issue
- Looking at the horizon, not just what is in front of you
- Seeing patterns that can inform your assumptions about how issues will play out in the future
- Drawing on your own and others' experiences to inform future decisions

Some of us rely a good deal on intuition and use it to help make decisions. Both intuition and vision are based on parts of ourselves with which we're not fully aware. Both provide insights into what makes sense or what feels right. If there are areas in which you have found your intuition to be particularly valuable, those areas are likely to show up in your vision. Some people trust their intuition when selecting employees. Others trust it about which products will sell or how fast to expand a business. For others, intuition is the primary driver for their vision of leadership.

Consider the following questions about how intuition might influence your leadership vision:

• What does your intuition tell you about your vision for leadership?
• How does your vision for leadership resonate with other people?
• Do you value and trust your intuition? Why is that?
• What has happened when you have acted on your intuition in your roles as a leader?
• In what situations has your intuition seemed most reliable? When has it been off-base? Can you discern what factors differentiate between being on target or off target with your leadership intuition?

Look Beyond Yourself

Finally, we strongly suggest you talk to others as you develop your vision for leadership. We believe that leadership is as much about collective activity as it is about an individual leader, and thus your own leadership vision is also connected, implicitly or explicitly, to the vision that others hold. As such, it's important that you be open to and seek input from other people. Our colleagues at CCL, Bill Drath and Chuck Palus, frame it this way.

> Our constructs of leadership, it seems, have been built up around
> . . . the powerful individual taking charge. This aspect of leader-
> ship is like the whitecaps on the sea—prominent and captivating,
> flashing in the sun. But to think about the sea solely in terms of
> the tops of waves is to miss the far vaster and more profound phe-
> nomenon out of which such waves arise—it is to focus attention
> on the tops and miss the sea beneath. And so leadership may be

much more than the dramatic whitecaps of the individual leader, and may be more productively understood as the deep blue water we all swim in when we work together [1994, p. 25].

As you think about your vision for leadership, consider the extent to which your vision aligns with and is influenced by the people with whom you work and serve and those you admire. Also consider the following questions:

- What inspires you about visions that others have about leadership?
- How can you build on and expand the vision held by others and make it your own?
- What is it that they want to accomplish, or what problem do they want to solve?
- Where does your vision for leadership fall short of the potential of the groups and teams with which you work?

In addition to looking for connections between your vision for leadership and the vision of members of collectives in which you participate, think about how and where you choose to concentrate your efforts in working with other people. Where and what you choose to focus on (or not) indicates something central to your priorities and to your leadership vision.

WHAT A CLEAR LEADERSHIP VISION WILL DO

At the start of this chapter, we defined vision for leadership as an ideal picture of what you might do as a leader. Therefore, as you develop a clearer vision of leadership, you'll clarify your direction as a leader—where you want to go, why, and what you'll do when you get there. You will make better decisions about the paths and options presented to you. You will know when you can and cannot compromise. You will better understand your passions and priorities. You will be better able to move toward roles that will allow you to express what you have to offer as a leader. You will know what you'd like to test or learn from future leadership opportunities. You will also find that clear vision lends a confident, steady sense of identity amid chaos.

In *The Unbearable Lightness of Being*, novelist Milan Kundera (1984) suggests that for everyone, there is an "*Es muss sein!*" ("It must be!"), that is, an overriding necessity that governs a person's life. This necessity will drive you toward a pattern in your ideas, needs, and passions. This necessity will also inform the way that leadership plays a role in your life. Through this process, you will gain insight into why some people find their way to leadership roles and others do not, by either choice or happenstance.

For some people, a desire for leadership forms part of a broader vision they have for themselves as humans. It's important to distinguish your desire for leadership from desire for simply power and influence. In *Good to Great*, Jim Collins (2001) writes about "level 5 leaders"—those who concomitantly hold as values a burning desire to succeed and a measure of humility (that is, they can attribute success to the contributions of others). In our work with many leaders from different sectors of society, almost without exception, the most effective leaders have combined a compelling vision with a burning desire to lead and a desire to assume responsibility for a higher purpose.

CONCLUSION

By now you clearly recognize the importance of a leadership vision to guide you through your choices and decisions as a leader. Reflect on the following final questions to see where you are in developing and articulating a clear leadership vision:

- What are you trying to accomplish through your leadership?
- What would others say about the guiding force for your leadership?
- If you were to outline the elements of your leadership vision, what would be included?

- Are the elements of your vision compatible or contradictory?
- How does your vision for leadership contribute to the success of other people, your team, or your organization?
- How does your leadership vision connect to your overall personal vision?
- What obstacles impede your enacting your vision for leadership?

New events, ideas, and ways of thinking will cause your vision to shift over time. At times of important transition in your life, you may wish to revisit the sources of your vision of leadership.

In Chapter Four, we move to motivations and values for leading—the third component of the Discovering Leadership Framework. If you still don't have a clear leadership vision, a look at your motivations and values will certainly help. Examining them will also give you more insight into why you feel adrift.

CHAPTER FOUR

YOUR LEADERSHIP MOTIVATION AND VALUES

Something about leading is important, motivating, or valuable to you, or you wouldn't be reading this book. Motivators are powerful forces. They compel you to action. Values are standards or principles that guide your beliefs, decisions, and actions. We believe that being aware of your motivations and values strengthens you as a leader and helps you clarify why you want to lead or why you are experiencing drift. This awareness can also help you choose among various types of leadership roles and derive more personal reward from your leadership work. Articulating your own motivations and values and understanding their role in your work as a leader isn't an easy task. Neither is figuring out if your motivations and values align with your current role or your organization's values.

This chapter describes five motivators for leading. It defines core values, where they come from, compatibilities and conflicts, and how they play out in behaviors and career choices. It sets out a broad range of values from which you can choose your own core values. The chapter concludes by describing the relationship of clear values, vision, and leadership.

YOUR MOTIVATIONS TO LEAD

Consider these questions as a backdrop to our discussion about motivation:

- What motivates you? Why do you want to lead? What experiences are you drawn to? What tasks give you energy?
- When do you find yourself in the zone and not drifting?
- When do you experience what Mihaly Csikszentmihalyi (1990) calls *flow*—those times when you are so absorbed in an activity that you lose your sense of time and place? Do you ever feel this way as a leader?

Motivation is about drive, enthusiasm, and inspiration. When we are highly motivated with our work, we look forward to the day ahead for what is on our plate to accomplish. Flow has a lot to do with motivation.

Each person's motivations are different, and the way in which they satisfy these motivations are different. We describe five sources of leadership drive or motivation: validation, rewards, impact, service, and meaning. One or more of these sources will likely explain what is pushing you to be a leader.

Validation

One manager told us, "Under the surface there's always been a bit of insecurity about whether or not I belong at the level I'm at.... As a result of this insecurity, I've been withholding part of myself in my business interactions, and that is actually seen as a problem."

Many executives come to CCL's leadership development programs wondering, "Is this when they will find out that I've been fooling people about my abilities? Is this when they will know I don't belong in this role as leader?"

Validation refers to the confirmations you receive that you can lead. Most people are concerned initially with whether they can be a leader at all or whether they can be a leader in a specific organization. Will others follow their direction? Will they be accepted as a person of authority? Do they have what is needed to take an organization to new heights? Are they motivated by the confirmation of other people?

Validation is crucial. It isn't difficult to imagine the impact on one new partner in a firm whom we recently coached. Her boss said that her greatest strength was her willingness and ability to take on the most complex, undefined, messiest challenges. Moreover, no other new partners he'd known had this skill set and desire.

Some people have received enough validation in earlier years. Others want the opportunity to continue to confirm their ability to lead in more complex situations and environments. How do you get that confirmation? If you are new to leadership, try experimenting in several leadership situations. You'll probably find that you can lead effectively at least some of the time. The feeling of "I'm okay" may come in a flash or gradually, or perhaps with qualifications and some developmental needs, but it's likely to be present in some degree if you pay attention to how you are feeling and what you are thinking. If you have already been leading, you may want to try new challenges that bring additional validation. As you take them on, listen for positive feedback. Do you receive confirmation that you have landed in the right role? Are you told about the value you are bringing? All too often, leaders focus too much on responding to negative feedback. By failing to embrace their assets, they can easily lose sight of the range of their abilities, from strengths to developmental needs. If this happens, a leader's strengths can become underused, which can lead to performance degradation.

Rewards

Some people are powerfully motivated by the typical rewards of a leadership position: prestige, status, respect, inclusion, recognition, money, and other remuneration.

Admitting to oneself or others that these are important is hard for some who enjoy these rewards but wouldn't publicly admit to being motivated by them. But some leaders truly are humble and don't care much about the perks. Among senior executives who have long enjoyed the rewards, some pay increasingly less attention to external rewards, while others see them as an automatic, natural outcome of carrying the leadership burden.

Nonmonetary rewards include training opportunities, exposure to top executives, travel, credit for projects, increased responsibility, opportunities for creative expression, control over their work schedules, and intellectual growth. Often these nonmonetary rewards can have more value than the monetary ones. In multiple surveys, workplace flexibility outranks pay as a benefit.

Do you know what rewards are important to you and how much of a driver they might be? What rewards are you currently receiving? Why are they of value to you? What other kinds of rewards do you desire? What will it take to achieve these? In Chapter Six, you will have the opportunity to look at these rewards or benefits in more depth.

Impact

The urge to make a difference is powerful. One hears this constantly during hiring interviews: "I want to have impact. I want to see the results of my efforts." One young bank vice president described to us the impact she wanted to have in clear and measurable terms: "Uniformity within the bank when it comes to groupware technologies—having a central place for the four hundred or so technical administrators throughout the bank to be able to come to know they're getting superior support, superior information. A pristine technology center is important to me, and getting a lot of respect from the people that ultimately come to us for guidance." People who have an impact, change things, and get things done garner respect. Leaders can achieve these things on a large scale.

Most of us spend our early years in organizations learning how to get things done with what we have learned in school and on the job and making individual contributions in areas such as technology, finance, and marketing. Then perhaps we are chosen temporarily as supervisors or given some duties along those lines. We start in such roles as crew chief, team leader, or "working manager," still making our own individual contribution. Eventually we slip into a role in which our individual technical contribution is small and our impact must come from being a leader. This transition is very important. Not all new leaders like what they find when they get there; some of them back out. Most professionals, however, find that they can shift gears and let go of their former ways of making an impact.

A leader's impact is quite different from that of technical experts, craftsmen, sales representatives, and other individual contributors. It typically comes through other people, which is what makes it potentially more powerful and gratifying. One leader we interviewed began her career in human resources and progressed through roles of expanding opportunity to make a broader impact:

> You start by [having an impact on] people at lower levels, just employees that need some help, that need to have someone in HR provide some guidance on a career perspective. I found that very satisfying earlier in my career. . . . When I got to a role more at the manager level, I started to get a little bit closer to understanding . . . what the business needs were and what the individual needs were. . . . Since then, I've really grown to be able to influence [other] managers, coming to the table with something to share and deliver.

Sometimes the leap from individual contributor to leader is less of a progression and more akin to being thrown into the fire. For example, a young business professor, recently granted tenure, was a member of the hiring team for her university's new associate dean, and the committee could not find the right qualified candidate. One day the committee happened to meet without her. When she subsequently joined the meeting, they told her they thought *she* was the best person for the job. After some consideration, she agreed to take on the job. Now she manages sixty faculty members in both the graduate and undergraduate schools of business. She took the role because she thought she could make a difference, and this thought takes her past occasional bouts of panic and uncertainty as she forges ahead to help reshape the university.

Is impact important to you? Why? What kind of impact are you having now? Is it the kind you wish to have? What kind of impact do you want to make in the future?

Service

A retail industry manager we know expresses his leadership motivation mainly in terms of service: "I lead from behind. I don't have a large ego; I don't consider myself needing the glory that comes with victories. I'd rather see myself with a group of people, behind a group of people, making it easier or possible for them to do the right thing."

To look back and see that we've helped others—made the world a better place by following our vision and doing the work—is often reported as the ultimate reward of leadership.

John Wood (2006) exemplifies service as a motivation. He was a senior executive with Microsoft, logging thousands of travel miles and spending long hours at his job. A transforming trek though the mountains in Nepal led to a significant life change and the start of Room to Read, a global nonprofit organization building schools and libraries in Third World countries. To date, his organization has served over 4.1 million children in eight countries and has a goal of reaching 10 million children by 2020.

Service is the foundation for servant leadership, a philosophy of leadership development associated with the work of Robert Greenleaf (1991). In contrast to a top-down hierarchical approach, servant leadership emphasizes collaboration, trust, empathy, and the ethical use of power. The leader is a servant first who keenly desires to serve others. The objective is to contribute to the growth of individuals through teamwork and personal involvement, so leadership is not about personal gain.

Some individuals who don't use the phrase nevertheless express it in their leadership style. This is often true of people who wish to be leaders in a just cause, as in hospital or medical organizations, environmental groups, political campaigns, or government agencies. Service may also motivate a leader who wants to help talented young women, fellow immigrants, people in her hometown, or some other specific group.

Do you find yourself motivated to help a particular group such as children, single moms, entrepreneurs, or teachers? When are you most attracted to serve? In what ways do you want to serve? Do you know others who are servant leaders? Do you want to be known as a servant leader?

Meaning

Wilfred Drath and Charles Palus (1994) write, "One thing we all share—across cultures, geography, and time—is the ability, and the hunger, to make things make sense" (p. 2). Some individuals seek leadership in order to find meaning for themselves and others. With increased learning and development, they gain greater clarity about life's meaning. One senior executive ponders, "How to craft a meaningful life over the next ten years? That is the essential question. I feel lucky to be able to sit back and give this issue thought and direction."

But meaning is elusive and evolving. Rapid change across our lives, organizations, and society often makes it hard to see. For reflective, continuously learning individuals, motivation to make meaning is a powerful drive in their leadership roles. It is meaning that turns a job into a calling or a passion.

A sense of meaning is one great antidote to drift. It can give you an overall sense of being in the right place. It can lead you to set high goals, make clear choices, and overcome obstacles. Meaning is often the reason individuals are able to transcend major hardships; they find meaning amid great tragedies.

Where do you find meaning? Have you lost the meaning in your current role? What makes you happiest? What makes sense about the life you have created for yourself? How and why have you ended up where you are now?

Synthesizing Motivation for Leading

It is important to understand your leadership motivations as best you can. Validation, rewards, impact, service, and meaning can all be sources of drive for leaders, giving them a sense of purpose, a rationale, or logic. Awareness of their importance to you will help you see where leadership fits into your life. What gives you energy, direction, and reward as a person will, in your leadership work, be a signal to others of what is important to you and what you value. In time, these forces can become the basis for the vision for an organization or community. Try to answer the following questions now:

- What motivations drive your leadership vision?
- How do you see these motivations operating in your current leadership role?
- What about being a leader doesn't motivate you?
- Where else do these five motivations play out for you?
- How might your motivations change with future leadership roles?

MOTIVATIONS AND CORE VALUES

There is a strong connection between what motivates you and what you value. In the following letter, written at the end of CCL's Leadership at the Peak program, a senior leader considers motivations and values:

> *Dear—*
>
> *Truly knowing oneself and coming to grips with what's really important to me, I suspect, will be the biggest take-away from this week-long course. Upon reflecting on "the really big question" my thought process continued to circulate around a few key themes like enjoying life, bringing enjoyment to others, and making a difference. These categories are broad yet very specific when I think about myself, my family, my organization and my community.*

Another leader from the same program writes this:

> *Dear—*
>
> *Sometime in the next 2–10 years you'll reach the summit of your current climb—you might be there now. The next valley and peak will likely be different. I don't think it will be characterized by wealth or prestige—maybe service but there's probably more.*

If satisfaction on that next peak is health, friendships and financial sufficiency then you need to maintain the first and last but work much harder on friendships. The current peak is characterized by experiences and service—those remain important but probably are not fully sufficient.

So, ask yourself today what you have done to work on friendships—if you are not on track then "look at yourself" and get with it.

Some motivations and values inform why you lead. Others inform a broader definition of what is important to you. They explain why you spend your time and energy the way you do, and why you feel conflict when your behaviors fall short.

Exhibit 4.1 is a fairly comprehensive list of common values (we invite you to add any others it may overlook). Analyze and prioritize the list for yourself. Reflect on how these values line up in relation to your behaviors. Look also for patterns of compatibility or conflict between them. Shortly, we will ask you to use this groundwork in identifying your core values.

EXHIBIT 4.1 COMMON VALUES

Achievement—a sense of accomplishment, mastery, goal achievement

Activity—fast-paced, highly active work

Advancement—growth, seniority, and promotion resulting from work well done

Adventure—new and challenging opportunities, excitement, risk

Aesthetics—appreciation of beauty in things, ideas, surroundings, personal space

Affiliation—interaction with other people, recognition as a member of a particular group, involvement, belonging

Affluence—high income, financial success, prosperity

Authority—position and power to control events and other people's activities

Autonomy—ability to act independently with few constraints, self-sufficiency, self-reliance, ability to make most decisions and choices

Balance—giving proper weight to each area of one's life

Challenge—continually facing complex and demanding tasks and problems

Change and variation—absence of routine; work responsibilities, daily activities, or settings that change frequently; unpredictability

Collaboration—close, cooperative working relationships with groups

Community—serving and supporting a purpose that supersedes personal desires, making a difference

Compassion—a deep awareness of and sympathy for another's suffering

Competence—demonstrating a high degree of proficiency and knowledge, showing above-average effectiveness and efficiency at tasks

Competition—rivalry with winning as the goal

Courage—willingness to stand up for one's beliefs

Creativity—the ability to discover, develop, or design new ideas, formats, programs, or things; to demonstrate innovation and imagination

Diverse perspectives—unusual ideas, opinions, and points of view that may not seem right or be popular at first but bear fruit in the long run

Duty—respect for authority, rules, and regulations

Economic security—steady and secure employment, adequate financial reward, low risk

Enjoyment—having fun and laughing

Fame—becoming prominent, famous, well known

Family—spending time with partner, children, parents, or extended family

Freedom—the power to act or speak without externally imposed restraints

Friendship—developing close personal relationships with others

Happiness—finding satisfaction, joy, pleasure, contentment

Health—physical and mental well-being, vitality

Help others—helping other people attain their goals, provide care and support

Humor—the ability to laugh at oneself and life

Influence—having an impact or effect on the attitudes or opinions of others

Integrity—acting in accord with moral and ethical standards; honesty, sincerity, truth, trustworthiness

Justice—fairness, equality, doing the right thing

Knowledge—the pursuit of understanding, skill, and expertise; continuous learning

Location—choice of a place to live that is conducive to one's lifestyle

Love—involvement in close, affectionate relationships; intimacy

Loyalty—faithfulness; dedication to individuals, traditions, or organizations

Order—stability, routine, predictability, clear lines of authority, standardized procedures

Personal development—dedication to maximizing one's potential

Physical fitness—staying in shape through exercise and physical activity

Recognition—positive feedback and public credit for work well done; respect and admiration

Reflection—taking time out to think about the past, present, and future

Responsibility—dependability, reliability, accountability for results

Self-respect—pride, self-esteem, sense of personal identity

Spirituality—strong spiritual or religious beliefs, moral fulfillment

Status—being respected for one's job or association with a prestigious group or organization

Wisdom—sound judgment based on knowledge, experience, and understanding

In *The Twelve Core Action Values*, Joe Tye (2008) defines a core value as "a deeply internalized philosophical guide that profoundly influences goal setting, decision-making, conflict resolution, and more generally how one lives one's life" (p. 1).

Your core values are the most important ones to you—the ones that drive your life decisions (relationships, jobs, places to live) and leadership choices (why you want to lead, what you want to accomplish). Becoming aware of or finding them is job number one, because they strongly influence what you pay attention to, how you make choices, and what you will defend in a conflict. One senior executive sizes up one of his very strong values—for better and worse—this way: "I have a very competitive streak in my DNA. I can come on very strong, and while some people may love my decisive, results-oriented, high-energy style, others are really put off. And I need to work at moderating the negative impact of that competitive DNA if I'm going to be most effective as a leader."

You may think that you already know your operative core values, but without having done any formal work on them, it's unlikely that you do. Articulating them can be extremely difficult and requires some honest, lengthy reflective time. You probably need to try several times before you can be sure.

Why is it difficult? It is difficult to choose among many good things—freedom, service, love, balance, collaboration, and advancement, for example. It is difficult as well to get away from social, political, cultural, or parental norms and similar outside pressures of thought. The reason is that most of us don't see ourselves very accurately, and how we live out our core values may change gradually over time. Sometimes we don't recognize a core value that led to some truly valued outcome or accomplishment. So, yes, this is difficult—but you can do it.

For businesspeople, some core values may relate mainly to accomplishments:

- Power, control, ambition
- Financial independence or success
- Helping people who deserve help
- Being a responsible person in family and community
- Working toward professional excellence
- Working toward entrepreneurial success

Other core values may have more to do with interpersonal relationships, within the organization (with peers, superiors, and direct reports) and outside it (with clients, stakeholders, and customers):

- Honesty and integrity in dealings with others
- Upholding the mission of the organization
- Respect for other people's needs and uniqueness
- Respect for the value of group decisions

Review the list of values in Exhibit 4.1 again. Can you pick out ten to fifteen as your core values? Write them down somewhere, and keep them handy as you continue reading this book.

Working Out Value Conflicts and Incompatibilities

In some situations, your core values may conflict, meaning that in a particular case, serving one may preclude another. At those points, it is helpful to write out the dilemma, talk to friends and colleagues, mull over the consequences of the various choices, or prioritize among those values. Learning from that choice can help you in making future choices.

One executive we spoke with talked about the excitement of being able to achieve partner in his firm (meeting values of ambition, financial success, and competence) but also the long hours and travel that kept him from spending time with his family (competing values of love and affiliation in this situation). Another executive noted that mounting pressures to do well at work (competence) denied her time to develop the less experienced members of her team (help others). Still another spoke of the conflict in terms of people skills that he values but abandons under performance pressures:

> I have people skills that a lot of CEOs would envy. But for a life-time I've worked very hard and I've been very goal-focused, very task-oriented. . . . As deadlines become more critical and their importance becomes more apparent, I tend to close out the good human relations skills and just become so task-focused that . . . some of [the people I work with] probably feel like they're being hammered. Others feel like they're being excluded. Some prob-ably feel like I don't care about them or their ideas or anything else. And they're probably right. . . . I need to be more conscious of what I'm doing and how I'm projecting myself.

Time is often short when important demands compete, and stress can lead us to operate in ways we later regret. Although you may not be able to eliminate such conflicts, it's important to know what they are in order to make the best choice possible or to articulate your dilemma to others. Here are some other examples to help you in your own reflection:

- Loyalty (desire to serve under someone) versus recognition (desire to stand out)
- Adventure (desire to explore) versus location (preference for a particular home site)

- Autonomy (desire for independence) versus affiliation (desire to belong)
- Competition (desire to win) versus collaboration (desire to cooperate)
- Order (desire for routine) versus spontaneity (desire for variety)

Do you see potential conflicts in your core values? Have you already experienced conflict? How did you handle them?

How Values Change over Time

Core values tend to be relatively stable over the course of our lives, although how we act on them may change, and what tops your list at age thirty might be lower down at age fifty-five. For example, early in our lives, we often take our health for granted. Later in life, we resonate with the statement, "If you have your health, you have just about everything." At different points, you might change the amount of time you spend in relation to one core value. At one point in your life, achievement might be always on your mind; years later, you might not value it quite so much and might value more personal time. You might also change where and how you demonstrate a value, perhaps moving it from a career setting into the domain of a hobby.

Think about the core values you held ten years ago, and compare them to your values today. What is different, and what is the same? To what do you attribute the differences? Perhaps a spouse or long-time friend can give you insights in this regard.

The Influences on Our Core Values

It is also useful to think about from where your specific core values come. From one of your parents? From a teacher, friend, coach, or mentor? Or does the value seem to reflect a norm of your surrounding culture? As an American manager, is individualism or entrepreneurship high on your list, in contrast to the Japanese manager who dwells on hierarchy and status? In addition, there are socially imposed values (those *shoulds* of life) that may not be conscious or important to us personally, yet we rank them high—for example, being considerate, helping others, or career advancement.

Our profession is sometimes an influence. You may have chosen to be a lawyer because of core values you already had, or that choice may have developed or strengthened a value you didn't always strongly espouse. Either way, it is likely that creativity is a core value for the artist, and duty is one for a police officer.

Your current context also influences the importance you assign to certain values. Has economic security become a higher priority for you in this global recession? Or, after devoting twenty years to your career and neglecting friends to some extent, has the value of friendship become more important? Clearly your organizational context has an influence as well (more about this later in the chapter).

In summary, where our values come from is influenced by our personal history, family, current context, vocation, and organization, to name a few key factors. It is always a good idea to stop, analyze, and reflect on the origin of your core values. Why are these values important to you? Where did they come from? Are they truly yours or someone else's?

Core Value Congruence with Statements and Actions

A deeper understanding of your core values comes by testing the congruence between a value and how you talk about it and act it out. Are what you say and do congruent with what you believe is important?

First, reflect on the principles by which you are actually living. At some level, you are deciding, consciously or not, how to spend your time, energy, money, and focus. Does how you are spending these valuable resources correspond with what you think you most value? If you value education and expertise, do you spend time learning, talking to other experts, and staying abreast of the latest advancements in a particular field? If you believe you value friendship, how often are you in touch with your close friends? While you may value helping others, when have you offered a helping hand?

You can also test your congruence by asking others about it. Often they are better able to see how you actually behave and what messages you actually send. You can poll friends, family, and colleagues about your values and how you demonstrate them.

Colleagues willing to tell you the truth are great sources of feedback about how you do or do not uphold and convey the values of your organization. For example, if innovation is paramount in driving its future success, do you publicly acknowledge innovative employees? Do you also provide coaching to those who need more help in learning how to innovate or money to support new ventures?

Personal congruence of belief, statement, and action is often called authenticity. Today employees want authentic leaders who are in touch with their employees, tell them the truth, and engage them in the organization's pursuits. They don't want leaders who toe the corporate line or mainly just pick up the latest jargon espoused in the latest business book.

Authenticity can awaken the passions of others and bring deeper emotional meaning to the work. In *Leading Out Loud* (1995) Terry Pearce calls this "speaking from the inside out": "Can leaders touch deeper values in themselves as well as in their audiences? Can they communicate practical solutions with greater substance and meaning?" (p. 23). Being in touch with your own values as a leader and able to represent the values of others and the organization are critical leadership qualities, enabling you to help others lead. As Tom Peters (2001) wrote, "Leaders don't create followers, they create more leaders" (para. 26).

One executive who attended Leadership at the Peak advised himself in this vein:

> *Remember H. Smith Richardson's philosophy that we need to develop leaders for the future (it's our responsibility). It's great to drive business, numbers are crucial and a great indicator of a great leader, but truly a great leader will do this and bring people to the next level of their career. You have a stellar group of executives working for you. Give them the autonomy to make their own decisions. Have confidence to trust their abilities to execute.*

But congruence must be accompanied by balance. Ron Heifetz and Marty Linsky (2002) write about the double-edged sword of overloyalty to particular values. How might overemphasizing a core value get in the way? For example, you may value responsibility, but might you also become overly responsible, taking on the problems of others rather than coaching them to solve the problem for themselves? Might you, because you value loyalty, stay in one organization or one part of the organization too long instead of diversifying your experience?

Core Values and Organizational Choices

There is no list of values to which all effective leaders subscribe and no one set for any given field, industry, or organization. But it is important to choose the field, industry, and, especially, the organization that you believe fit your own core values.

Most organizations have well-defined values; they might be the written values hung on a wall at headquarters or printed in an annual report, or the unwritten values that show up in the behaviors of staff and are reinforced by company culture. Employees may be unable to tell you what the written ones are, but they'll know the unwritten ones. Do you know the stated values of your organization and the extent to which they align with your own values and the behaviors of the people in the organization? When you work in an organization that has fundamentally different values, both your job satisfaction and ability to lead are likely to suffer. Consider this remark from one executive, known for taking risks, who was hired to help an organization surpass its cautious, conservative ways: "The company is not necessarily rewarding my kind of behavior. They talk a lot about taking risks, but they don't reward that behavior. They reward the success but not the risk. So if you take a risk and it doesn't quite work out, there are consequences."

Dealing with Possible Risks

Many of the leaders we have talked to described values conflicts with their organization that led to significant personal risk. Fortunately, their awareness of their own values generally kept them in contact with their principles and led them to decisions that did not damage their careers. Here are two examples.

The Strength of Clarity A manager in an energy company was a valued troubleshooter who reported directly to the president. He says the president had "kind of brought me along with him.... I learned a lot from the man. He had a lot of raw, natural talent, very little formal or business training." But a conflict eventually arose as the president started exhibiting a very unethical side:

> I would try to steer him away from these types of situations. Finally, one night I received a call from the chairman of the board, who asked me some very direct questions about things that were happening. I chose to be honest with him. As soon as we got off the phone, the president called and said, "I hear you just threw me to the wolves." ... I didn't get fired, but it strained the relationship considerably. I stood up. I didn't back down. I wasn't apologetic.... The conflict was, on the one hand, wanting my security and taking care of my family and, on the other hand, sticking my neck out and trying to help the business.

In this case, we believe that the manager acted consistently with his values. What allowed him to do so was his clarity about his own values, which gave him the strength to deal directly with both the chairman of the board and the president, to whom the manager felt a personal debt.

Despite Regrets A financial officer worked for a while with a start-up that wasn't getting off the ground. Then he looked at two other possible jobs. Of the first he says:

> I thought it was a nice job, and I liked their values. I spent a lot of time, went to meetings, I was really wooed. They had a problem that they needed to solve. I spent a great deal of time looking at their sense of purpose, corporate values, how they communicated with each other, worked in teams, and I thought this was great. They wanted to know about me, and I wanted to know about them too. [But] the decision-making process in this company takes a very long time.

Then suddenly the second job came up:

> It was a pre-IPO situation. I said, "Thank you, Lord, this is it!"
> I've always wanted to take a company public. I'd have a good
> title, comptroller, I'd be on the SEC [Securities and Exchange
> Commission] report and all these wonderful things. I interviewed.
> The company was making money hand over fist.
>
> So I turned down the other company and said I'd take the
> position with the IPO. The VP of finance was a Harvard grad,
> and I had a lot of respect for him. Then I interviewed with
> other people in the company. I had questions about some of
> the other people. They didn't seem as strong as I felt they should
> be, given the fact that this was going to be a public company under
> a lot of scrutiny, and there was tremendous risk. Well, after going
> to work for them I found that the only people who had college
> degrees were people in the finance department. It took about three
> or four weeks to find out that this was part of the culture—that
> they devalued education and people who had education. There
> would be a lot of snide remarks about my boss for no other reason
> than that he had his Harvard degree. And when I talked about
> education, taking courses for myself, my staff, and so forth, I
> heard, "Well, we don't do that. We don't value education."
>
> Then I went to staff meetings and saw how people operated.
> None of it was illegal, not something that would get you thrown
> in jail. But I was having a tremendous value clash here. I was
> thinking, "All your life you've stood for integrity and dealing with
> people below you fairly. . . . You're not going to be able to do that
> here. You're just going to have to take the money and not look
> after your people."
>
> Finally, I just went back to the other company and said, "Is
> that job still open?" I did this just four weeks before the [second]
> company went public. I walked away from a lot of money. And
> that had been my whole goal in life: a whole lot of money.
>
> I do have regrets, thinking, "Gee, you could have made a
> lot of money." I do [wish] I had the money for education for
> my kids and stuff. But what would you learn, [having] all those
> stock options but [being] in conflict every day? And would this

organization hold that over me and manipulate me and make me unhappy? Probably. Or if not me, make my staff unhappy, and then I'd have to live with that.

Again, despite the element of regret, we think this person made the right choice in the long run, based on clear though sometimes opposing values. Certainly these situations are not easy.

Shifts in Organizations' Values

As organizations' structures and climates change, so do some of their values. For example, when an organization decides that a strong team environment is critical to its future, it will likely look less favorably on independence or autonomy. Conflict often results when an individual in this environment can't become a team player and continues to stress the older values.

Understanding whether your values match those of the organization is more challenging in the current climate of mergers and acquisitions where multiple value systems operate within the same organization. That understanding is harder to come by also as the nature of the workplace changes, as we noted in Chapter Two. As organizations shift employment strategies to contract employees, telecommuting, global partnership, and the like, the sharing of values may be harder. It may not even be realistic to expect high compatibility between your values and the organization's values. The best result may be to find compatibility with your boss and your immediate work group instead of the overall system.

In sorting out the fit between your values and those of your organization, we suggest you share your values with others, even your boss, and talk with them about values. If people are transparent and understanding about value differences between you and them, less conflict may arise in the future.

In summary, as you continue navigating your values and career:

1. Understand the traditional, current, and emerging core values in your field (or industry) or a field in which you are thinking of working.

2. Know which values are rewarded in your current or prospective organization, and know the values of its key leaders (including the boss and peers).

3. Be clear about the core values that you associate with your concept of a good leader.

4. Assess whether your core values match items 1, 2, and 3.

VISION AND VALUES

So what is the link between leadership vision and values? Let's begin with a remark from Charles Handy, cofounder of the London Business School, who writes that "the vision cannot be something thought up in the drawing office. To be real, it has to come from the deepest part of you, from an inner system of belief" (quoted in Pearce, 2003, p. 18) This inner system holds your values.

Core values provide the meaning behind our leadership vision; they direct it. Knowing them gives insight into why we dream the way we do, what we fear, what we hope to accomplish, and how we want to live our lives. Two men who connected vision and values when they founded their company are Ben Cohen and Jerry Greenfield, who shared a common dream since their high school days in the 1960s on Long Island and now are famous for the ice cream that bears their names. Along with ice cream, the two friends valued friendship and the kind of hope that seemed to be circulating in the air of the United States in the 1960s. Other values high on their list and reflected in their leadership included the following (Cohen and Greenfield, 1997):

- *Creativity.* There's often a better way; there's no need to just live with tradition.
- *Equality.* Everyone likes to feel important; hierarchy subtracts from good relationships.
- *Social responsibility.* Successful people must give back to their workers and the community.
- *Quality.* Only the best will do.
- *Fun.* It's not worth doing if it isn't fun to do.

Think about the leadership you envisioned in Chapter Three. What values are embedded in it? What values do you want to be known for?

Clarity of Your Values

Why give so much attention to values? For much the same reason that we dwelled on vision in Chapter Three. Clear and conscious values inform why you do or do not want to be in a leadership role, the kind of leadership role you choose, your style of leading, what motivates you, what to do when you experience conflict, and how you go about making decisions. Clarity about values also gives you insight into reasons for drift. Clarity has many benefits:

- *Clarity of values guides leadership behavior.* Warren Wilhelm (1996), vice president for corporate education at Allied Signal, says that effective leaders increasingly will be those who are aware of and act on their values: "Leadership without direction is useless. Uninformed by ideas about what is good and bad, right and wrong, worthy and unworthy, it is not only inconsistent but dangerous. As the pace of change in our world continues to accelerate, strong basic values become increasingly necessary to guide leadership behavior" (p. 222).

- *Clarity of values guides leadership choice.* A clear value of service (desire to serve) led one senior publishing executive in her mid-forties to leave her firm to become the executive director of the local Habitat for Humanity. A recognized desire to feed her creative side led a finance officer to start a community theater on the side. An elderly parent's failing health led a couple to move across the country and seek leadership roles in Omaha, Nebraska. A director of research with a growing desire to understand how diverse global perspectives work together moved his family from the United States to Singapore. Thus, our values can guide our leadership choices over time into new interests, careers, locations, or networks.

• *Clarity of values speeds up decision making because right answers are more readily apparent.* For example, if good health is important to you, you won't take long to choose between fried or grilled chicken. If diverse perspectives matter to you, you won't delay soliciting all viewpoints on a problem. Clarity helps you choose with conviction, and when this choice yields good results, the value is reinforced.

• *Clarity of values helps you know when you act incongruently with your values.* In small or big ways, you will feel personal conflict: "I shouldn't have said that." "I should have done that." "I shouldn't have made the decision." Such feelings help you know when you are off track. As Joe Tye (2008) explains, "The more conscientious you are about living these values, the more successful you will be at achieving your most important goals, and the happier and more fulfilled you will be as a human being" (p. 2). Who doesn't want that?

• *Clarity of values will help you know if your values really match the organization's values.* We know that an organization's value system, evident in organizational culture, is sometimes stronger than its strategic, structural, or operating system. A good match is critical for supporting the work you want to do and the way you want to lead. A senior executive with a training and development organization left to take a larger role within a prestigious research and training firm. The role was perfect. But soon after arriving, she learned that the organization's values were really built on what was good for the CEO. Everything had to be run by him—every letter, every decision, every meeting, and even the scheduling of a dentist appointment. The work was just what she wanted, and how she was able to serve her constituencies was even better. Yet her position became unbearable.

• *Clarity of values helps when you encounter conflicts among values.* Recently we worked with a group of midlevel managers from a variety of organizations on strengthening their role as leaders. One of the participants admitted to disliking his role and longed for the opportunity to return to the role of an individual contributor. He didn't enjoy the managerial responsibility for others: development plans, setting performance goals, or dealing with their personal challenges. He much preferred being a technical expert helping clients solve major issues. Why was he staying in the role? He stayed because his family was used to the financial rewards that accompanied his position. Through his decision making, he placed a higher value on his love and loyalty to his family and their needs rather than his own job satisfaction.

In another example, the needs of a colleague were in conflict with the needs of the organization. An executive was leading a new product development group with high pressure, high visibility, critical deadlines, and resource constraints, and the product was running behind schedule. Then the project manager for a new key product, which was behind schedule, asked for a week off. The demands of the project kept him working seventy hours a week, and he had neglected his family. Tension had arisen with his spouse, and he needed time to salvage the marriage. The executive shared this family value but also valued high quality, which included on-time results, and there was no one else to replace this manager in lean times. The executive worried over how to help the manager without putting his own job on the line. The problem was hard to resolve. After multiple conversations and shifting of other people resources, they were able to the meet the deadlines and give the manager the time that he needed.

An organization's values can also conflict: its financial health versus job security for employees; managing an organizational partnership that has collaborative and competitive components; conservatism or risk in times of economic uncertainty. Often the best answer is situational and requires considerable analysis.

These situations of tough calls and lack of clarity over the right decisions are common. Leaders often face choices between seemingly equally important values. By knowing their own values well, they can more readily identify these conflicts and work to find optimal solutions.

Will life be kind to you, handing you only leadership questions with obvious right answers? Probably not. With today's complexity, no one right answer may exist. You may just need to apply your values and judgment to finding the best solution. Often only hindsight will tell whether the decision was right. Did I take the right job? Did we invest in the right product? Open the new office in the right location? Form the right partnership? Sell off the right business? This is always complex work; when values compete or conflict, it's even harder.

Right and Wrong Values for Leaders

It is tempting to try to name appropriate and inappropriate leadership values. Isn't it always better to be fair, loyal, or honest? Can manipulative, autocratic, narcissistic, greedy, or selfish people be effective leaders? We'd like to answer yes and no, but we've seen situations in which the latter people are nevertheless considered reasonably good leaders.

We can report on one case study of leaders who led their companies to success. In *Good to Great* (2001), Jim Collins reported on companies and their leaders who sustained outstanding performance over multiple years. He found that all of what he called "level 5 leaders" valued two qualities: professional will and personal humility. These leaders were ambitious—but for the company, not themselves. They were self-effacing and understated. They were driven to produce results and took responsibility for any mistakes but widely shared any credit. From this study and what we know from Enron, WorldCom, Arthur Andersen, Bernie Madoff, and the various recent political scandals, it appears that taking action and making decisions based on personal gain and ego is how leaders lose their way.

Whether there are right and wrong values for leaders may not be the question to ask. Some tried-and-true values, such as honesty and integrity, do guide good and great leaders. But there isn't one right way to be a leader. The same goes for values. There isn't one right combination or set of values that determines how effective a person will be as a leader. What matters is that leaders understand and can manage multiple sets of operating values: their individual values, the values of others for whom they are responsible, and the values of the organization. Conflict will arise among these three sets of values and will need to be sorted out. To manage this complexity, you must know your own core values and how they guide your choices.

CONCLUSION

This chapter has described motivations and values in order to help you know more about yourself, why you may be experiencing drift, and the role that values play in your leadership and the rest of your life. We encourage you to continue talking with trusted colleagues, friends, and relations who can help you understand these relationships more clearly.

Reflect on the following questions to see how motivations and values play a part in your leadership choices and life decisions:

- Why have you chosen to be a leader?
- When are you most satisfied as a leader?
- If someone were to ask you about your core values, what brief summary statements would you give them?
- How are your core values reflected in the way you lead?
- What conflicts are you experiencing in relationship between any of your core values?
- How are your motivations and core values connected to your leadership vision?

In Chapter Five, we ask you to look beyond your conscious values to your leadership profile. We concentrate on your personal styles, competencies, responses to change, and work experiences. Studying these aspects of yourself will help you explore your feelings of drift and determine how best to take action.

CHAPTER FIVE

YOUR LEADERSHIP PROFILE

We have been encouraging you to make more conscious choices about why, when, where, and how you lead. Chapters Three and Four helped you to investigate the why. In this chapter we shift to the when, where, and how. Where and when do you like to lead? How do you lead, and what parts of that are hardest for you? The answers lie in your leadership profile. The profile defines you further as a leader and tells what you bring to leadership roles.

Having this knowledge about yourself can help you find your way out of drift, or even avoid it altogether. You will look for roles that use your strengths or add value to your portfolio of experiences. You will better understand your response to change or your need for collaboration within your team. You will better understand why you feel stuck or what you are looking for next. Discovering and understanding your leadership profile will help you work from a place of strength as well as understand gaps in your set of skills.

As you read this chapter, keep these four important hows in mind:

1. How to lead in a way that is you and not someone else
2. How to call forth the right leadership skills in a given situation (this is the art of leadership)
3. How to prevent fatal flaws from derailing you
4. How to set yourself up for success by having the necessary experiences or assignments.

If you master these four, you will open doors for future success. The key is knowing yourself.

After discussing why it is important to know your leadership profile, the chapter surveys its various components and helps you identify and describe more fully who you are as a leader. Think of your profile as a leadership tool kit to draw on as necessary. Your tools are leadership competencies, leadership roles, learning styles, experiences, and more.

THE USE OF A LEADERSHIP PROFILE

In the late 1980s, Peter Vaill (1989) introduced the notion of management as a performing art as opposed to simply knowledge and skills that could be obtained by memorizing and applying formulas in a linear manner. He wrote, "One mistake the arts would never make is to presume that a part or role can be exactly specified independent of the performer, yet this is an idea that has dominated work organizations for most of the twentieth century" (p. 124). We believe that Vaill's idea about art and management also applies well to leadership. Great managers use their whole selves, infusing their work with their own multifaceted, complex character and personality. For some people, the organic connection between person and leader seems obvious. But it can take years to grow comfortable with the notion that strong leaders are the ones who are being themselves and acting in character as they fulfill their leadership roles. To be yourself, you must get to know yourself rather than, say, trying to be all things to all people.

Yet CCL researchers Corey Criswell and David Campbell (2008) have found that many very senior executives have a need to define and maintain a rather narrow executive image and "unnecessarily put tight limits on themselves, trying to maintain a powerful façade, when revealing their personality and humanness is a better sign of effective leadership" (p. 12).

The Importance of Knowing Your Profile

Knowing your leadership profile lets you be more agile and flexible as you lead, aware of how you can best contribute in various situations. You know when to step forward and when to step back and listen:

> Self-aware and reflective executives do not simply accumulate knowledge and expertise; rather, they call upon the right capabilities at the right time. Such executives perform more effectively because they adapt better to the particular situation; they are more flexible. The more aware they are of what they can and can't do, the better able they are to deploy themselves in an enlightened way [Kaplan, Drath, and Kofodimos, 1991, p. 30].

Knowing your leadership profile also makes you more insightful in working with others about how your behavior affects them, and it affords a better understanding of yourself as a stimulus and influence. Knowing your profile also helps you recognize the diversity of styles, experiences, and needs of others and to address difficult issues with them. Aware of your own needs and interests, you're less likely to unintentionally compromise the needs, interests, and motivations of others.

Knowing your leadership profile will help you understand how experiences increase your learning. Mistakes and hardships teach us the most. After her very visible and painful downfall at Hewlett-Packard, Carly Fiorina wrote in *Tough Choices* (2006): "Life isn't always fair, and I was playing in the big leagues. Yet I realized I had no regrets. I had completed my mandate. I had made mistakes, but I had made a difference. I had given everything I had to a company and a cause I believed in. I had made tough choices, and I could live with their consequences. While I grieved for the people and the purpose I had lost, I did not grieve for the loss of my soul" (p. 306).

Your Strengths and Weaknesses

Along with knowing your profile comes the challenge of accepting and using what you know. By accepting who you are, including your limitations, you can acknowledge to yourself and others where you can shine and where you need help. You can also work on weaknesses or pair up with others who bring compensating strengths.

Leadership research has tried to determine whether it's better to focus solely on your strengths (Buckingham and Clifton, 2001) or to work on strengths *and* weaknesses. In fact, a good assessment will probably show that many of your qualities fall in the middle—neither clear strengths nor clear weaknesses. With that in mind, we recommend focusing on both your strengths and weaknesses without overly fretting about limitations. What to do with your strengths? First acknowledge what they are, and work to truly understand what behaviors of yours embody them. Then either simply draw on them as needed or look for better ways to leverage them or develop them further.

But also try to assess whether any weakness—or development need—might become a factor in derailment. Longstanding global research at CCL has found that five main factors derail executives; we look at each later on in detail. As soon as you can, address that weakness or potentially fatal flaw. For lesser needs, determine which you would benefit from working on, which can be left alone, and which warrant finding a team member to supply. Your choice will likely be based on current and long-term personal and organizational priorities and the amount of energy you or others can give to the effort. We have found that too many leaders spend an inordinate amount of time on weaknesses at the expense of leveraging strengths. When this happens, you end up with mediocre performance because you underuse your strengths.

YOUR PERSONAL LEADERSHIP PROFILE

We consider six elements essential to a leadership profile:

- *Leadership competencies.* What do you bring to leadership?
- *Leadership roles.* What roles do you like to play?
- *Learning styles.* How do you learn?

- *Change styles.* How do you respond to change?
- *Developmental assignments, career history, and life experiences.* What experiences and lessons do you bring to leadership?
- *Derailment factors.* What gets in your way? What have you failed to learn?

As you read, think about how each element of your profile might contribute to your current state of drift or one of being in the zone.

If you've already participated in an assessment-for-development leadership program like those offered at CCL, you have a wide array of information to draw on about yourself. Self-knowledge may also come from formal self-exploration or organizational feedback, such as performance appraisals. Another type, 360-degree feedback, involves systematically collected opinions about a manager's performance from a wide range of peers, direct reports, supervisors, customers, suppliers, board members, and other parties. All of these data will be helpful to you as you move through the chapter. If you have not yet had any formal feedback, this may be a good time to seek it.

Leadership Competencies

Leadership competencies are skills and abilities that leaders need to carry out leadership tasks. Many companies are now building their own list that they use for promoting, developing, and rewarding employees. Through customized 360-degree instruments, they measure how leaders are doing on the list. In his goal-setting letter, one senior executive referred to his 360-degree feedback and focused on four competencies he wanted to improve:

> *First, . . . increasing my social interaction and energy level. This will involve*
> *several specific actions. It will include more walking around and getting out*
> *of the office . . . more face to face and oral discussions (i.e. cut back on email)*
> *. . . more story telling . . . more talking with peers and employees about matters*
> *outside of work—such as learning some new personal information about each*
> *one of my direct reports.*

> *Second, . . . inclusive empowerment and delegation. This will involve seeing a broader array of views from our team on important matters . . . listening more before providing my opinion on a topic . . . spending additional time in a project to provide more guidance.*
>
> *Third, . . . employee development. This will include spending more time on work assignments to ensure key performers are getting high profile projects . . . a meeting with each direct report and specific key performers on their personal and career desires, separate and apart from our semi-annual performance reviews . . . also getting my direct reports before the executive committee more.*
>
> *Fourth, . . . changing approaches to resistant peers. This will include, when time permits, more face to face time with such peers to raise issues and concerns, as well as to ensure they present all facts in an unbiased manner.*

We believe that the following eleven competencies are foundational (always important) and critical (contextually important) for leaders today:

- Demonstrating integrity
- Building trust
- Getting things done through others
- Developing others
- Communicating well
- Building teams
- Technological savvy
- Comfort with ambiguity and uncertainty
- Flexibility and adaptability
- Creating networks and alliances
- Global astuteness

For each, think about how you have seen it in action and how others might rate your performance. Add any you think we have overlooked—competencies that are critical to your role or are rewarded in your organization. Recognize also that these competencies are not always distinct and separate; often they are interrelated. For example, getting things done through others is also a means of developing others.

Demonstrating Integrity

Integrity is about doing the right thing. Leaders who tell the truth and are reliable breed trust. They are careful to avoid conflict of interests, they answer the tough questions honestly, and they also hold confidences. In these ways, they garner respect from their colleagues. Integrity can be tough to maintain in the face of power and politics.

Building Trust

Building trust with people from varied backgrounds, specialties, work styles, cultures, genders, races, aspirations, and generations is not an easy task. If you want their best efforts, their best thinking, and their passion for excellence, you must earn their trust and confidence. Your knowledge and ability will impress them far more than your title. Some contributors to trustful relationships are fairness, genuineness, a willingness to learn from errors, respect for each other's talents and needs, and a willingness to listen.

Getting Things Done Through Others

You have undoubtedly heard the phrase, "It takes a village." Important and complex work goes beyond a single individual or a single leader. A leader needs to know how to work through others to achieve results. Therefore, a leader needs to be able to assess the skills of his or her team, have patience to help them grow and develop, and be willing to share the credit.

In our interviews, we asked the regional director of a national retail chain, "What do you think is the toughest job of a leader?" His immediate response was, "Patience with your people and patience with yourself. You might do something better than someone else, but three people can do it better and faster than you can. So you have to let them learn how to do it and let them understand how to do it." He freely admitted that patience did not come naturally to him. He had to learn it as he went along: "I think a leader who looks for glory, [who] is always out front of his people, gets frustrated in the leadership role because people recognize that and will not support that person in bad times. I've found that those kinds of [leaders] pass blame."

Developing Others

Developing others takes time and investment. It means creating a developmental plan for those for whom you are responsible and committing yourself to keeping the development of others as one of your top priorities. This plan would include giving them access to challenging assignments to help them learn and grow. As a developer of people, you would also be assessing their strengths and development needs and providing continuous feedback. Support is critical, as are listening well, offering to be a sounding board, affirming their hard work, and helping them learn from mistakes.

Communicating Well

In light of all of the contextual changes described in Chapter Two (different organizational structures, different generations, more demanding customers, globally dispersed teams), communication skills cannot be overemphasized. They start with knowing your constituencies and being able to engage them through your powers of speaking, writing, and listening. You need to master the do's and don'ts of public speaking, videoconferencing, teleconferencing, client presentations, written communications (memos, e-mail, blogs), and one-to-one conversations. Effective leaders of global, flexible, and widely dispersed organizations place a premium on the abilities to be heard and understood and to hear and understand others.

Building Teams

One executive completed a leadership development program with this goal in his mind:

> Build a team! You never really knew how to go about it until
> now, but it's actually fun! You've done a great job of surround-
> ing yourself with top-notch people. Pull them together, and make

it your business not to be the one with the answers. Instead, try
to help them find answers of their own. Then use and enjoy what
they give to you.

Teams are composed of individuals or groups with different skills
and styles—and often conflicting agendas—sometimes working across
geographical regions, time zones, and functional areas. Important team-
building subskills are setting direction, understanding group cohesion,
clarifying team roles, confronting conflict, giving feedback, building
morale, fostering open dialogue, and providing appropriate support
and structure. The last task—supporting the team as a whole as well
as each individual member—can be huge. Creating a structure that
rewards team effort is mandatory for reinforcing the motivation and
incentive to work as a team.

Technological Savvy

In the "old days," many in positions of authority relied on
administrative assistants to facilitate, produce, and distribute various
communications. Today, with leaders at all levels and work dispersed
among teams that often cross cultures, countries, and time zones,
technology is playing an enormous role. Leaders today can no longer
distance themselves from technology. You need to know how to proactively and purposefully use the various technologies to facilitate work,
be they Skype, Twitter, Webinars, Facebook, LinkedIn, videoconferencing, personal digital assistants, global positioning systems, or the
next new thing. Technology is a key to an organization's competitive,
strategic, and operational direction and a driver of an individual's
success.

Comfort with Ambiguity and Uncertainty

Uncertainty is inevitable, and ambiguity is ever present. You will
want to cultivate enough comfort with them that you even prefer
to work on the edges of stability and predictability, seeking out the
ambiguous. Leadership is often about navigating gray areas. It is also

about positively using the forces of change, making decisions without all of the data you'd like to have, and being comfortable with reasonable levels of risk. To do this well requires self-confidence and a certain amount of interpersonal agility and resilience.

Flexibility and Adaptability

The pace and degree of change today mean that your focus at work may well be different in eighteen months. You may be in the same role within the same organization, but the structure of that organization, those you are working with, and the responsibilities you hold could be different.

Al Calarco and Joan Gurvis (2006) conclude that "adaptability is no longer a nicety or a coping mechanism. Adaptability is a leadership imperative" (p. 8). They cite joint research between CCL and George Mason University that found three components of adaptability: cognitive flexibility (use different thinking strategies), emotional flexibility (being aware of one's own emotions and the emotions of others), and dispositional flexibility (remain optimistic and realistic at the same time). A leader who is able to demonstrate all three is well on the way to mastering this competency.

Creating Networks and Alliances

The executive director of a national nurses' organization told us: "I've loved helping nurses get the education . . . support and networking that [they need to] feel good about the patient care that they give. The network of the people I know has really come to be one of my most important resources—putting the right people together in the right room so they can help each other. For me, leadership is building new networks all the time."

Networks and alliances are benefiting individuals, teams, and organizations more and more. Curt Grayson and David Baldwin (2007) suggest that developing, maintaining, and using contacts is the heart of leadership networking. These relationships allow you to share resources, support, data, and rumors (also important!). They also allow you to build up credits with people in useful places that you can cash in when you or your team needs help. Networks help you stay knowledgeable about power shifts in the organization.

Networking requires skill in creating, nurturing, and maintaining relationships. The good news is that social networking platforms such as LinkedIn and Facebook facilitate connections. They foster finding similar interests, matching needs with solutions, and staying current with one another.

At the organizational level, networks, alliances, and partnerships are critical for expanding into new markets, providing unique or bundled services, or innovating. Instead of building up internal capacity, organizations are seeking partners that give them advantages without making tremendous demands.

Global Astuteness

Many papers, articles, books, and research studies note a continuing shortage of people who know how to lead and manage in the new global context. Individuals who seek global opportunities and learn how to integrate across cultures, geographies, and languages are highly marketable. Global astuteness is the ability to manage the complexity of time zones, the business practices and norms of different countries, the nuances and meaning of language, the diversity of social identities, and the communication and feedback patterns of different cultures.

Synthesizing the Competencies

Is this list of competencies complete? Certainly not. Nevertheless, it's a good beginning for your discovery process. Reflect on the following questions:

- Would you add any other competencies to the list of leadership skills?
- Which of these competencies do you consider your strengths?
- Which of the competencies are more difficult for you?

- What have you done to develop competencies in areas in which you are weak?
- What are the most important competencies in your current role?
- What competencies do your boss and organization value most?
- Which of these competencies will be less important in the future?
- Which of these competencies will be more important for you in the future?

Your Leadership Roles

By "roles" we don't mean the position you hold, such as chief learning officer. We mean functions or parts you play, formally or informally, depending on the situation or needs of the broader organization. Leaders must be able to recognize, span, and use a wide variety of roles. Exhibit 5.1 provides a list of roles that practicing leaders often see and mention.

EXHIBIT 5.1 COMMON LEADERSHIP ROLES

Advocate	Facilitator	Mediator	Organizer
Astute observer	Fixer	Mentor	People developer
Change agent	Implementer	Motivator	Problem solver
Coach	Innovator	Negotiator	Risk taker
Collaborator	Integrator	Networker	Strategist
Communicator	Learner	Nurturer	Team or community builder
Entrepreneur	Manager	Ombudsman	Visionary

Some roles may come naturally to you, and you take them on easily. Others may seem more difficult, and you avoid them. You don't need to be good at all of them, but you should know which roles are your strengths and which are needed in a given situation. If you can't perform one of them well yourself, someone else on your team or in your department probably can.

Organizational culture influences which types of roles are more or less valued and noticed, and the relative importance of different roles shifts as an organization matures. For example, in a start-up or entrepreneurial venture, visionaries, innovators, and risk takers play the most prominent roles. Later, those who think more about systems and processes, such as organizers and managers, tend to be desired. When an organizational culture begins to overemphasize a particular set of roles, it is common for neglected ones to received renewed attention.

Consider the following questions:

- What roles are currently valued and rewarded in your organization?
- What roles are devalued or often absent?
- What roles are most important to your organization's future?
- What other roles come to mind that aren't on this list? Go ahead and add them.

Now think about yourself in relationship to these roles:

- Which three roles do you do best?
- Which three are most difficult for you?
- Which of your three best roles are integral to your work?
- Which roles do you value most?
- Which roles are you being asked to play by your boss and direct reports? For roles you don't play well, are there individuals from whom you can learn?
- Is there a role you must play that is contributing to your challenge of drift?

Do you see any alignment between your responses here and your core values or motivations for leading you discovered in Chapter Four?

Your Learning Styles
In this world of fast-paced change, leading well is all about learning. CCL research has shown that we learn the most by using a variety of learning tactics (Dalton, 1998). But personality and how we process information influence how we prefer to learn and narrow the ways we choose to

learn. You can challenge this by noting and using different learning tactics, thereby gleaning more from every developmental experience.

Let's examine four sets of learning tactics: action, thinking, feeling, and accessing others. First, you'll need to understand where your preferences lie among the four and identify possible upsides and downsides of each. Then you will want to understand how you can expand from your preferred, more comfortable tactics to others. The result can be greater effectiveness as a leader.

Action Tactics

This is learning by doing—by direct experience. These learners confront a challenge head-on and hands-on, in real time, and figure it out as they go along. The action tactician is a risk taker—a person who gets down on the factory floor and makes on-the-spot decisions in a crunch. In this frame of mind, learners do not feel that gathering data from others first is necessary. The downside is that they may not have all the information they need and could get before they act. Or because they haven't consulted others, they may be repeating others' mistakes. And in some leadership situations, they may ignore others' feelings and reactions and perhaps never gain their commitment.

Thinking Tactics

These tactics involve working things out by oneself. These learners recall similar or contrasting situations. They reflect on the past, imagine the future, and play out scenarios. They gather information from books and reports to ground themselves well in the facts. These individuals don't risk being caught uninformed. The downside of an overused thinking style can often be procrastination, overintellectualizing an issue, or not engaging with others who can or help refine a plan. Others may view those with a strong thinking style as preferring to lead from their office, their e-mail, and the phone rather than engaging with others.

Feeling Tactics

These are used by learners who manage the anxiety and uncertainty that comes with new challenges. They can acknowledge the impact of their feelings on what they do, trust what their intuition is telling them, and confront themselves when they know they are avoiding a challenge. If you learn this way, you may isolate yourself unnecessarily from others who have different perspectives. Feelings can often paralyze, yielding inaction and indecision. Or you can overreact to emotional components and resist reason or data that can counterbalance the feelings.

Tactics for Accessing Others

With these tactics, people seek advice, examples, support, or instruction from others who may have coped with a similar challenge. These learners may learn how to do something by watching someone else do it or by taking a useful course or program. Downsides to accessing others too much are that you may be avoiding your own feelings about an issue; you may overdiscuss instead of act; you may become overreliant on others and not look inward to your own thoughts and self discovery; and you may be sending signals to others about your lack of readiness or incompetence regarding some leadership task.

Understanding Your Learning Style

To understand your learning style, reflect on the following questions:

- Can you identify your preferred learning tactic?
- Which learning tactic do you least prefer?
- How does your preferred learning tactic benefit you?
- How does it benefit others?
- How might you and others benefit by expanding the use of these learning tactics?
- How does your learning tactic relate to drift? (No time to think? Lack of access to the right people? Inability to take action for fear of making a mistake?)

By becoming more versatile and using all four learning styles, you can learn more from the challenges and experiences you face and be ready to take on the more complex and senior roles in your organization.

Your Change Styles

Change is endemic to a leader's life. Sometimes change happens to us, and sometimes we create it. Leaders need to develop comfort with change and ambiguity. But just as learning tactics differ, so do styles related to change. Of the three we will consider, none is better than the others; each has its strengths and limitations.

Chris Musselwhite and Randell Jones (2004) set out a continuum of differences in how individuals respond to change. At one end stand the Conservers, who react to change by working on it through their current reality and structures. At the other end stand the Originators, who prefer to try new approaches. In the middle are the Pragmatists, who tend to view change situation by situation, focusing on getting things done with whatever strategies work.

You can imagine how these different preferences can be the source of tremendous power (different ways for teams to solve an issue) and considerable conflict (teams with no common language). You need to be aware of your own preference and how it interacts with those of your boss, peers, and direct reports; when to leverage your style; and when to draw on the preferences of others. As you read the descriptions, think about which one describes you best.

Conservers

People with this style prefer change that fits within existing systems and structures and are excited by improving or building on what is already there. They enjoy predictability and a secure work environment. They also honor tradition and established practice. Conservers are strong at helping others stay focused on the mission and what is working. To others, they appear disciplined, organized, and deliberate. Their pitfall is being seen as too cautious, inflexible, rigid, detailed, and resistant. To help with these perceptions, conservers can work on exploring alternatives and acknowledging possible advantages of new ideas or opportunities.

Pragmatists

People with this style see the merits of both improving existing systems and identifying a new desired outcome. They can often map the steps needed to get from current reality to a future picture. They focus mainly on solving problems, balancing inquiry from the other styles to reach an optimal solution. To others they appear cooperative, collaborative, and flexible. A pragmatist's pitfall is being viewed as indecisive, wishy-washy, self-serving, and easily influenced. To help with these perceptions, pragmatists can develop criteria by which to evaluate all ideas, make sure they state their own opinions, and give themselves a deadline for making a decision.

Originators

People with this style are excited by new opportunities, possibilities, and ideas. You will often hear them purporting a new vision for the future, biased toward action. They prefer quick and expansive change. To others they appear to be risk takers, change agents, and idea people. The pitfall is that originators may be viewed as impulsive, undisciplined, and ignorant of their impact on systems and people. To help with these perceptions, originators can make sure to communicate what they see as currently working, prioritize among the number of good ideas, and create realistic time lines after checking available resources.

Understanding Your Change Style

Reflecting on these questions will help you identify and understand your change style:

- Do you prefer one of these change styles?
- How does that preference benefit you? Others? Your organization?
- What are its pitfalls for you?
- Have you seen conflict result from differing change styles?
- Is your drift related to not being valued for your approach and response to change?

Insight into your change style can help you better understand your strengths, the impact you have on others, and why certain perceptions exist.

Developmental Assignments, Career History, and Life Experiences

In interviews for a new position, the interviewer often says, "Tell me about a time when you successfully navigated a difficult situation," or "Tell me about a time when you delivered some tough feedback." These questions are meant to draw out your experience—what happened, why it was significant, and what you learned from it. From your experiences, you may have gathered a wealth of information, wisdom, and expertise applicable to future work. All experiences can teach us: in developmentally useful on-the-job assignments, in our career progression through different organizations, or in our broader life experiences.

Developmental Assignments

Cindy McCauley (2006) reaches three key conclusions about leader development:

- Throughout their careers, effective leaders continue to develop their repertoire of skills.
- Much of this development comes through practical experiences.
- The more varied the practical experiences are, the greater the likelihood is of developing a broad repertoire of skills.

McCauley's approach to learning is referred to as development in place because individuals don't have to leave their jobs, attend a course, or wait for promotion to continue their learning. Without doing any of these, they can simply add challenges that broaden their experience or target a specific competency.

In order to decide what challenges would broaden your experiences, inventory your past work experiences. What events had a lasting impact on you as a leader or manager? Take the time to describe as many of these events and what you learned from them as you can. Then reflect on what is missing. Seeing the gaps, you can plan how to fill them.

CCL research has identified ten job challenges that commonly lead to executive learning:

1. *Unfamiliar responsibilities*—handling responsibilities that are new or very different from previous ones you've handled
2. *New directions*—starting something new or making strategic changes
3. *Inherited problems*—fixing problems created by someone else or existing before you took the assignment
4. *Problems with employees*—dealing with employees who lack adequate experience, are incompetent, or are resistant to change
5. *High stakes*—managing work with tight deadlines, pressure from above, high visibility, and responsibility for critical decisions
6. *Scope and scale*—managing work that is broad in scope (involving multiple functions, groups, locations, products, or services) or large in sheer size (for example, workload, number of responsibilities)
7. *External pressure*—managing the interface with important groups outside the organization, such as customers, vendors, partners, unions, and regulatory agencies
8. *Influence without authority*—influencing peers, higher management, or other key people over whom you have no authority
9. *Work across cultures*—working with people from different cultures or with institutions in other countries
10. *Work group diversity*—being responsible for the work of people of both genders and different racial and ethnic backgrounds

Now reflect on these questions:

- Which of these experiences are included in your work history?
- What did you learn from them?
- Does your current or prospective leadership role include any of the ten?
- Which challenges are missing from your portfolio of experiences?
- Do you have too much, too little, or the wrong kind of challenge right now? How is this contributing to drift for you?

CCL has also discovered the lessons that specific experiences teach. If you are struggling with a particular leadership competency (such as how to lead change or admit mistakes or confront a problem employee), you can find an appropriate matching experience to help you develop the leadership competency you need.

Career History

Looking at your career history is another way to appraise your repertoire of work experiences, examining the kinds of positions you have held, what you have learned, what parts of your experiences you liked and didn't like, and how it all informs your leadership. Douglas Hall, Kelly Hannum, and John McCarthy (2009) write: "Diversity of experience is at least as important as depth of experience. An individual who has been exposed to and has worked in multiple functions, varying roles, or multiple companies may be a better candidate in today's business environment than someone who has done one thing well for a single company for a long time" (p. 21).

Examine your career progression from the start:

- What decisions led you from one position to the next?
- How proactively did you seek new opportunities?
- Did you ever ride the sea of change and later regret taking a position? Do you regret not taking something that was available to you?
- When in your career were you most satisfied? When least? What were you doing at those moments?

Also, describe the leadership components of each position you have held:

- Were you, for example, a change agent or a nurturer?
- What specific leadership lessons did you learn in that position?
- What did you like most about performing a certain leadership role? What least?

- What are the leadership components of your current role? What would help you be more successful at doing these well?
- What would you like to do more of? Less of?

Then focus on four leadership problems in which you had the greatest impact. Consider also the impact of others who were working around you:

- How did you know you had an impact?
- What makes these career moments memorable for you? What did they teach you about yourself?
- What leadership experiences are missing from your career history? Should you try to incorporate any of them? What significance could they have in your career progression?

Asked these kinds of questions, the managers we interviewed offered refreshing insights and confessions. One said, "I think the things I've done were more managerial than truly leadership." Another had these words:

> I've learned that I'm not comfortable taking risks. It's just not in my comfort zone, and it's something I need to continue to challenge. Also, I don't like conflict.... I like to build a relationship, and I'm really good at team building and motivating.... I'm good at ... setting a vision, setting some direction without micromanaging.... But I don't like to deal with conflict, and sometimes I need to push back.

In contrast to that manager, another leader we worked with said:

> Companies tend to throw you into that management spot. I got there because I was a great technician, not because they saw me exhibiting great management skills.... It was a good two to three years before I started feeling somewhat comfortable at being the manager. Suddenly every decision I made not only affected me

but ten or twelve other people.... I think one of the most difficult things was to learn those people skills and be comfortable confronting people on performance issues and those kinds of things.

My personality tends to be very strong. I think it's good, and I want the rewards. But I want to be very careful that ... I'm not in this just for me. We've got a group that has to survive here. If I keep getting promoted up the ladder and my team is staying where [it was], then I don't feel like I've succeeded. Is it a discomfort for me to have the limelight? Not in a million years, but I'd feel even better if they were with me.

Life Experiences

Powerful personal experiences outside work can transform who we are, what we pay attention to, what becomes important, and how we decide to lead. Maybe you don't feel you have had a significant personal experience but you have had experiences that have likely shaped you as a leader. Reflect on your life, and identify any experiences that you believe are relevant to your leader development. What happened, and what did you learn? How have these experiences made you the leader you are today? Capture this as part of your larger leadership profile.

Derailment Factors

So far we have focused on the experiences, competencies, roles, and styles that have contributed to your growth as a leader. In this process, you have identified what you do well and areas for improvement. We turn last to some behaviors or gaps that can totally block a leader's success. CCL has done extensive research on derailment—what happens when individuals on the fast track are demoted, fired, or reach a plateau in their career progression. Leaders can fail to meet the expectations of the organization when they are unable to adapt to new demands and complexity in a leadership role.

CCL researchers Bill Gentry and Craig Chappelow (2009) identify five factors that have emerged consistently in derailment studies since 1983: problems with interpersonal relationships, difficulty leading a team, difficulty changing or adapting, failure to meet business objectives, and too narrow a functional orientation.

Problems with Interpersonal Relationships

This factor is frequently mentioned. Some managers who are poor at relationships are described as insensitive, manipulative, critical, demanding, and untrustworthy. Others are said to lack a teamwork orientation. Senior executives describe them as being solitary, a "lone wolf" and not a team player, and unable to communicate.

Difficulty Leading a Team

In some managers, executives see "no human skills" or "bad people management." Here is how one senior executive perceived one manager's problem: "He overworked his team both physically and psychologically. He expected them to work long hours and, instead of showing appreciation, he minimized their work and their contributions. As this behavior continued, people became more and more reluctant to work with him. He became isolated, and he tried to use his power to threaten them."

Difficulty Changing or Adapting

In the face of a changing environment, a person may be unadaptive, inflexible, and narcissistic. Executives may call managers who cannot change "absolutely egotistical" or "pig-headed." Such people are likely to hold on to old ways of doing things, be unable to handle more strategic roles, and fail to adapt to new structures or cultures.

Failure to Meet Business Objectives

Some people have difficulties following up on promises or completing a job. They neglect critical work, don't finish work, or self-promote with nothing to back their claims. They can also be overwhelmed by complex tasks and overestimate their own abilities.

A Narrow Functional Orientation

This derailment factor refers to a lack of depth, or failing to take an expansive view toward key organizational issues. This is most often true for managers who moved up the organizational ladder in the same functional area such as marketing. When given responsibility for much broader cross-functional areas of the organization, they derail. As a senior executive described one individual, "He was promoted to director because there was nobody else to take the position at the time. His analysis was very limited, and he made major mistakes and flops. He was not competent enough for the position."

Do any of these derailment factors resonate with you? Have you received information or feedback before on any similar behaviors that might suggest a trouble spot? Have you seen others in your organization derail for these reasons?

Derailment occurs for two main reasons. One is that some leaders do not understand their own strengths and weaknesses and how strengths can become weaknesses; this problem can be mitigated by continuous feedback. The second is that some leaders are aware of their strengths and weaknesses but are unwilling to change. For these leaders, change will come only when they see the merits of change or wish to avoid the consequences of not changing.

Derailment is a significant problem. It can harm the individual and the morale of coworkers, and it can cost the organization. As the talent shortage looms, preventing derailment becomes even more critical. However, derailing does not mean someone can't get his or her career back on track. Recovery and new maintenance depend on seeking feedback and help from others.

CONCLUSION

This chapter gave you the opportunity to examine your leadership profile. We hope that you have new language and new thoughts in your tool kit. And we hope too that you have identified some things that you need to develop to add to your repertoire of learning and lessons. Reflect on the following questions to see what else you might uncover about your leadership profile:

- Do you see any patterns among your responses to the seven elements of the profile?
- Do the patterns suggest some signature strengths—those that make you a valued leader?
- Do the patterns give you insight into why you are either drifting or in the zone?
- What are two key areas in which you might develop?
- How would you summarize your leadership profile?

As you reflect on your responses to these questions, do you see links back to the chapters on vision and on values? Do some patterns emerge in your leadership profile?

In the next chapter, we visit the fifth, and final, topic in our framework for discovering the leader in you: your personal context and how it, like your work context, influences and shapes your leadership. Once you have studied your personal context, you will be ready to explore strategies for achieving a more integrated and rewarding life in which leadership plays a significant part.

CHAPTER SIX

PERSONAL REALITIES, DEMANDS, AND EXPECTATIONS

I n Chapter Two, we described how current organizational realities affect the availability of leadership opportunities, the demands on leaders, views on leadership, and the costs of leading. In this chapter, we look at personal realities and expectations that surround and influence your work as a leader. Roles, responsibilities, and experiences from your personal life inform what kind of leader you want to be, how much time and energy you dedicate to leadership, and what roles you might accept or decline. Many lessons you learn in your personal life can transfer to your work as a leader. However, conflict between the priorities of work and home can often lead to drift or prevent you from taking action to get out of drift.

In this chapter, we examine the interdependencies of work and personal life and see how each arena shapes and influences the other. We also present some strategies for managing the various priorities in your life. The ultimate aim of the chapter is to help you resolve any conflicts so that you achieve the right amount of focus, energy, and time among the areas of your life in order to be a more effective leader.

IMPACT OF WORK ON PERSONAL LIFE—AND VICE VERSA

As complex work demands more hours and more energy, as technology has allowed twenty-four-hour connectivity wherever you are, as plane, briefcase, home office, or temporary work space all become your "place of work," and as you change jobs, organizations, and industries throughout your career, work life can easily infiltrate more of your personal life. When this happens, it becomes difficult to distinguish between your time and effort at work and at home. (Indeed, we wrote most of this book while at home.)

With fewer boundaries between work and home, multitasking rises, and the stress of trying to achieve work-life balance increases. In addition, work stress and its health care costs have risen drastically. When we talk to executives, we increasingly hear them lament the loss of quality family or personal time and the difficulty disconnecting from work due to the electronic gadgets they carry with them wherever they are and whatever they are doing.

Impact of Work on Your Personal Life

Here's a typical pattern. Driven by the normal rewards and expectations of work life (for example, to become more financially secure or gain greater recognition), you give more time and energy to work. The return is often greater financial rewards, greater responsibility, and more pressure to work even longer hours. Soon work spirals beyond control. Locked in this cycle, you too easily neglect family commitments or other aspects of your personal life, especially if they do not provide as much positive affirmation as your job does. Quite often leaders don't see this pattern developing until the situation explodes.

At the same time, economic pressures, layoffs, mergers, acquisitions, and other stressors cause the organization to demand more work from fewer people. So people works longer hours to keep their jobs or frantically try to reinvent their careers for higher pay when their spouses are laid off. This too takes a toll on personal lives.

A leader's own values, needs, wants, and drives also can contribute to the impact that work has on one's personal life. This comment from a senior executive illustrates the point:

> In the summertime, there have been times when my husband
> has called me at 8:30 or 9:00 [in the evening], saying, "Are you
> going to come home?" I just completely lose track of time because
> I actually enjoy what I do; I get into it, and it's fun for me. [But]
> when I hear my son tell his friends that the only way he can reach
> me is to text me, then I know that I'm going overboard and really
> have to back off. That's been a hard lesson.

Before we move further into the content of the chapter, step back and consider the following questions. Be completely honest with yourself as you reflect on each one:

- How has work affected your life outside work over the past year?
- What have been the benefits of work to your development as a leader and as a human being outside work?
- What have been the downsides?
- What is your biggest challenge in finding time for other roles outside work?
- What satisfies and dissatisfies you about the impact of work on your personal life? Have these factors contributed to your feeling a sense of drift?

Impact of Your Personal Life on Work

Just as leadership work affects personal lives, the reverse is also true. Our personal lives encompass numerous roles (for example, parent, spouse, son, friend, PTA president, grandparent) that lead us to additional responsibilities (for example, college tuition, home mortgage, retirement savings, school projects, laundry, grocery shopping). Our personal lives can affect how much money we want or need, how we choose to use our time, how much responsibility we seek, and where our energy goes.

Asked, "Are you putting your sights on a particular VP job higher in the organization?" one corporate director responded: "No. And I'll be quite honest. I am not willing to give up my family at this point. I just know what others at the vice president level give up. And I'm just not willing to make that sacrifice."

In addition to personal roles and responsibilities, we all have expectations that stem from our life philosophies and experiences. Our family of origin, generation, nationality, religion, and personal experiences all shape how we act as leaders in the workplace. Whether your father or mother was a traditional breadwinner, a stay-at-home parent, or not present very often, these factors have influenced who you are as a person and as a leader. If you grew up in a multigenerational household and were raised in Norway, you might lead differently from someone from the United States who was raised in a one-parent home.

Family of origin and other factors in your family context are parts of your social identity. Social identity encompasses three general components: given identity, chosen identity, and core identity (Hannum, 2007). Core identity refers to the attributes we believe make us unique as an individual—for example, traits, behaviors, values, and skills (which we discussed in Chapters Four and Five). Given identity is the characteristics we are born with or given to us in childhood or later in life (for example, gender, nationality, skin color, height, birth order). Chosen identity refers to choices around our relationships with others, where we choose to live, and the social groups we choose to join.

Our given identity—where we are born, Asian or European, male or female, short or tall—influences how we lead as well as how others perceive our leadership. Likewise, where we choose to live, the family makeup we choose or experience (for example, divorce, marriage, blended families, single, gay), and our profession (for example, engineering, education, law) shape our lives, our social groups, and our behaviors as leaders. Also, as we highlighted in Chapter Five, these factors, as well as unchosen significant life experiences, can influence our attitude toward work, our beliefs about good health, and our outside interests or passions. All of these in turn can have an impact on our leadership.

Before reading on, take a moment to record some notes on these questions:

- What parts of your given identity have influenced you as a leader, and in what ways?
- What about the influences of your chosen identity?
- What other priorities exist for you outside work? Do they contribute to or get in the way of your effectiveness as a leader?
- What life experiences outside work have influenced your behaviors as a leader?
- What general views of life have contributed to who you are as a leader?
- All things considered, how would you characterize your work-life balance?

Keep these responses near you as you read about some key topics of connection between work and personal lives.

WORK-LIFE INTERDEPENDENCIES

Now that you more fully recognize the influence that work has on personal life and vice versa, let's take a look at a long-standing integral tension: how to effectively balance your personal and work lives. Advice about work-life balance shows up constantly in popular magazines and business periodicals, on television talk shows, and in various other media addressing all kinds of audiences. This issue draws so much attention because it continues to be a vexing problem for many people, and especially for leaders.

Most often, *work-life balance* refers to tensions of time between work and one's personal life. As individuals have wrestled with this issue, many conclude that achieving balance is an unrealistic goal, while others redefine the dilemma as something other than measuring how to divide time (Hammonds, 2004). In a 2009 speech, Jack Welch told the Society for Human Resource Management, "There's no such thing as work-life balance. There are work-life choices, and you make them, and they have consequences" (Tuna and Lublin, 2009). As one CEO aptly put it to us, "I hate the balance concept because it means that every day I'm going to be a perfect mom and a perfect chief executive. Impossible. Simply impossible."

We agree with these points. Achieving work-life balance is unrealistic if we define it only as an issue of allocating time. Although how and where you spend your time is important, you also need to understand the benefits of the tension between work and home, what activities in either sphere give you energy, and how attending to the right priorities at the right time can increase your leader effectiveness. For each person, the picture looks different. You need to decide what balance is for you and use strategies that fit your own needs.

Changing Views of Work-Life Balance for Leadership

Before we move to strategies, let's take a deeper look at this topic of the tensions and interdependencies of work lives and personal lives. All senior leaders have days when they feel like a tightrope walker who is juggling multiple plates and trying not to drop any of them. Long hours, tiring travel, needing to get more accomplished with fewer resources, as well as increasing demands of working in a global environment conspire to deny leaders a sense of being in control. Most senior leaders, regardless of age, gender, or race, find themselves grappling with these choices of focus, energy, and time.

For example, in the United States, balance was once viewed as only a working mom's issue. Journalists and surveys still commonly report how working mothers spend their time, suggesting that mothers often still have a tougher time than fathers at finding a healthy balance. For many historical, social, and psychological reasons, mothers are still expected to, want to, or have to shoulder more than half the work of parenting. But this trend is shifting with more dual-income families and as more fathers become stay-at-home dads.

One of life's tensions for both men and women is that the tasks of building a family and building a career often occur simultaneously. These roles come into conflict when energy and time are important to performing well in both roles: leader at work and parent and spouse at home. When male CEOs at CCL's Leadership at the Peak program are asked about their greatest stress, the most frequent answer is loss of time with family versus a challenge they are facing at work. At the end of one CCL course, a senior executive, in a letter to himself, worked the problem through in the following way:

> You've known all along it's all about balance. You've had it rein-forced this week. That realization came to you over 10 years ago when all you had was your career. That lack of balance in your life was killing you. You had nothing left for yourself. What little you were able to muster for your family was utterly inadequate and almost cost you your marriage.
>
> Over the last ten years you have gained some ground by taking some of the focus off your career and refocusing some of your energy on yourself. You still haven't improved your relationship with your family.
>
> You now probably have a fair balance between your career and yourself, but your relationships with your family, friends and coworkers are a far cry from where they need to be. Your prioriti-zation skills stink. How could you let ten years go by and still not have your relationships in balance with the rest of your life?
>
> You are 52 years old and your kids are in college. You are running out of time. In fact, you don't have another 10 years to work on it. You have to do it now.

> onths I want you to focus on repairing
> nportant relationships in your life. Your
> e on your family. The kids will be difficult,
> . You'll have to pick up the pace with
> t it is a must you develop those critical
> vas very evident this is the major item to
> tly, please maintain the few close friends
> ng to need them.

other than work is a problem for men hose who are married and have children. ;e for all types of leaders, including heads of households, single parents, leaders just starting their careers, and leaders with a few years left before retirement. Imbalance is an equal opportunity player.

Another shift we see is that younger generations aren't buying into the constraints to which older generations submitted. They demand more flexibility, more choices, and fewer trade-offs. If asked, many will say they do not want to work the way their parents did, particularly if they saw their parents sacrifice a lot for an organization that only lengthened the workday or ended up terminating their employment.

So why is imbalance such a big issue? It's an issue because of the stress caused by multiple competing priorities that lead to long days, too little sleep, guilt, worry, and resentment. Without ways to relieve stress, energy fades over the long haul; the stamina isn't there to overcome real obstacles; and ambitions fall prey to ill health. These problems all contribute to the challenge of drift. As one executive wrote:

> I was involved in so many different things that I really didn't have
> any time for myself. I lost sight of who I was. I got to a point where
> I was just getting up every day, and people would wind me up and
> I'd just go. I didn't know what day it was, where I was supposed
> to be. It was like I was driven by an appointment book. So I had
> to shut down. I actually shut down for about six months before
> I started getting reenergized and back into activities.

When you are rightly focused and attending appropriately to the multiple parts of work and personal life, you see ways to achieve your ends, and energy can flow more freely. Thus, your effectiveness as a leader depends in part on your ability to balance or integrate your career and family obligations, your community and social lives, the pursuit of learning, and whatever other priorities you have in your life. Each part of life makes legitimate demands, and each offers important nourishment. Achieving some semblance of the right focus lets you lead with a fuller heart and soul. Effective use of your whole self allows you to go beyond tactical leadership and into strategic or transformational leadership. This is not just opinion but is grounded in research.

Are Balanced Leaders Really Better?

Two of CCL's multirater (360 degree) assessment instruments include items for comparing effectiveness with balance. The Skillscope questionnaire (Kaplan, 1997, p. 3) asks raters whether the person being assessed "strikes a reasonable balance between his/her work life and private life." The Benchmarks assessment (Lombardo and McCauley, 2000, p. 26) asks for responses on the following items: "Acts as if there is more to life than just having a career; has activities and interests outside of career; does not take career so seriously that his/her personal life suffers; and does not let job demands cause family problems."

In administering these instruments to hundreds of thousands of leaders and their raters, we have found that when executives received high marks from their coworkers on these specific items, the high marks on balance were not associated with lower marks on overall leader performance. The executives were considered productive, proactive leaders of the organization despite the time they carved out for their family, community, or other external endeavors. In one study using 360-degree data, managers who were rated higher in work/life balance were also rated higher in career advancement potential (less likely to show signs of career derailment) than managers who were rated lower in work/life balance (Lyness and Judiesch, 2008).

CCL research on women found that multiple roles nourished rather than hindered careers. One study of 222 high-achieving managerial women showed that commitment to four key roles—home care, parental, marital, and occupational—contributed to better work performance and to life satisfaction and higher self-esteem (Ruderman, Ohlott, Panzer, and King, 2002). Also, women committed to multiple roles were rated higher by bosses, peers, and direct reports on organizational skills, interpersonal skills, and personal awareness than women committed to single roles. Moreover, women single-mindedly devoted to work were rated lower as collaborators and were viewed as unduly pressuring coworkers. A subsequent study of 346 male and female managers found that commitment to family roles and spousal or life partner roles had a positive impact on job performance (Ruderman, Graves, and Ohlott, 2007).

Delving further into balance as defined by having "interests and activities outside of work," we find a slew of articles on exercise, nutrition, energy, and stress and their connection to effective leadership. Sharon McDowell-Larsen (2009), CCL's resident exercise physiologist, found that senior executives who exercised were rated significantly higher on overall leadership effectiveness in multirater assessments than their nonexercising peers.

David Rock (2009) demonstrates that stress-filled situations interfere with the brain's ability to function well. When we are under stress, we have less oxygen and glucose available, our memory gets cloudy, we have trouble thinking nonlinearly, and we have less capacity to solve complex problems. Essentially stress can reduce one's memory and performance and interfere with the ability to fully engage in the activities at hand, whether at work or at home. Finding ways to reduce or deal with stress is thus essential to leadership performance.

Tony Schwartz (2007) argues against managing one's time to fit in exercise, relaxation, or stress reduction activities. He suggests that organizations should focus instead on helping individuals sustain their capacity or energy because "greater capacity makes it possible to get more done in less time at a higher level of engagement and with more sustainability" (p. 64). Schwartz employs a variety of strategies for boosting energy and is able to measure positive bottom-line business impact for a financial services organization with these strategies.

Thus, studies point to potential positive results for both leaders and their organizations from interdependencies between our work and personal lives and from spending time outside of work on other priorities.

The Benefits of Lesson Transfer

Further study of the interdependencies between work and personal lives shows additional connections and benefits. For example, important lessons are learned in each arena of life that can benefit the other.

Research at CCL examined how interactions among roles can contribute to a high-achieving woman's professional and personal development. From the women's personal lives, six significant skills and benefits were identified as increasing effectiveness at work (Ruderman, Ohlott, Panzer, and King, 1999):

- *Interpersonal skills.* Women gained experience in understanding, motivating, and respecting others.
- *Handling multiple tasks.* As a result of juggling personal tasks, setting family goals, and so forth, women were able to multitask effectively.
- *Leadership skills.* Leadership opportunities in community or volunteer settings provided lessons about leadership in the workplace.
- *Psychological benefits.* Increased self-esteem and confidence developed in the women's personal lives helped them feel confident professionally.
- *Emotional support and advice.* Getting support from family and friends helped women succeed at work.
- *Personal interests and background.* Pursuit of personal interests and cross-cultural experiences or background brought value to women's work.

Often more value is placed on the learning that one does at work, but clearly lessons in personal life are valuable and transferable. The trick is to become aware of these important lessons and then capitalize on them. One executive described the learning and interactions between herself and her husband that had implications for a more flexible leadership style at work:

> In the partnership that I have with my husband, I think we trade
> off on leadership roles. We balance each other very well, to the
> point where we have somehow adapted to and adopted some of
> the personality traits of one another. I've typically been more
> of an extrovert, my husband a little less so, but over the years I've
> seen the benefits of not being quite so extroverted and I think my
> husband has done the same in just the opposite [direction].

Reversing perspective, we hear many executives describe positive effects of work life on their personal lives. They mention the financial rewards of individual advancement: access to the good things in their personal lives—the kind of home they want, children's education, and flexibility to spend long weekends with their family. For some, this includes opportunities to travel to interesting parts of the world, the chance to integrate business trips with family vacations in special places, opportunities to have lots of interesting friends and acquaintances, and the ability to call on a broad array of networks when needed.

Patrick Lencioni (2008) notes the discrepancy between the proactive time and energy we put into running our organizations and the reactive, chaotic mode in which we often handle our family lives. He provides lessons on how to take what we learn from work and apply these lessons to our families.

Organizational Responses to Issues of Balance

In recognition of the vexing problem about balance and wanting to retain talent, some organizations have changed their policies to embrace leaders as more complex, more integrated persons. One large management consulting firm that we've worked with has started a program that allows employees to "dial up" or "dial down" their career if they need less travel or client service, want to move laterally into a new role, or want to ease toward retirement.

As organizations compete for talent, many are looking at the benefits they offer to recruit and retain high-caliber leaders in whom they invest time and money. These benefits include gym memberships, on-site day care, and flexible work arrangements, all of which help employees manage complexities in their lives. Of course, the idea is that productivity will increase as well. Google's flexible benefits are renowned for their flexibility and enticement:

- Up to eight thousand dollars a year in tuition reimbursement
- On-site medical and dental facilities, oil change and bike repair, valet parking, free washers and dryers, and free daily breakfast, lunch, and dinner at eleven gourmet restaurants
- Unlimited sick leave
- Twenty-seven days of paid time off after one year of employment

- The Global Education Leave program that allows employees a leave of absence to pursue further education for up to five years and $150,000 in reimbursement
- Free shuttles equipped with Wi-Fi from locations around the Bay Area to headquarter offices
- Classes on subjects ranging from estate planning and home purchasing to foreign language (French, Spanish, Japanese, and Mandarin)

For some organizations, the purpose of additional benefits is to reduce the organization's health care costs, which are driven up by stress and by time away from work due to illness. Gym memberships, on-site fitness rooms, and incentives for physicals to reduce insurance costs are intended to help reduce medical bills for the organization. The good news is that these efforts benefit the employee as well.

Now look at your viewpoint on leadership and balance:

- How does an interdependent perspective on your work and personal life play out for you? Do you see connections to leadership? In what ways?
- Is work-life balance a topic of conversation in your organization?
- What have you seen change in individuals and organizations over the past five years as they address the impact between work and personal lives?

YOUR OWN WORK AND PERSONAL LIFE SITUATION

Our goal is to help you achieve the right amount of focus, energy, and time among the various areas of your life so that it benefits you as a leader and those you lead. Begin this process by examining your thoughts and assumptions:

- Is balance about having enough time across all of the areas of your life?

- Is it about analyzing how you spend time and adjusting allocations?
- Does a solution lie in reframing how you think about work-life balance?
- Do you define "work" as your formal, paying job and not consider your stints on a school committee, at church, or on a community board as work?

Another assumption we all make is that working harder and faster and multitasking make us more effective leaders. True? As noted earlier, Tony Schwartz (2007) helps challenge the assumptions, rules, and norms that govern our personal and work lives. For example, is it productive to respond to every e-mail? Schwartz says that the switching time in multitasking undermines productivity: constantly shifting attention from one task to another lengthens the time to finish each task by 25 percent. Challenging our assumptions and looking at information from different points of view can be helpful in solving or at least minimizing the turbulence we feel.

Also ask related questions. What puts your life out of balance? What is missing from your life? Is it that you need to spend more time with your kids, to read a book for pleasure, to travel, to finish a major work project, to read business books, or to exercise? Asking what is missing might point you to something you can change to improve your work satisfaction, and in doing so, you find more energy and benefit to your life more generally.

If you haven't already figured this out, the answers to the questions we pose above are core to the process of discovering the leader in you. Each reader of this book faces a different context and thus will answer these questions differently. One CEO we met summed up his answers in a poignant letter to himself:

> *You are . . . standing at the threshold of an introspective crunch. You have a choice as to whether you find joy or not in your time ahead.*
>
> *You have had a successful career and have achieved more than what was expected academically and in your jobs, but the same methods and practices that have ensured your success [up to now will not work any more].*

Your "babies" are now 6 and 10. How many days do you spend real time with them? How do you want them to remember you? Are you a source of nurturance at all times to both of them and their mother? Where will you find the time? You have a choice.

Your work life is packed from sunup to sundown. You complete all the paperwork, reports, requests, return calls and emails, but did you move the company somewhere new today? Did you simply go down your list of items with each supervisee or did you ask them a single question that just might open up their thinking?

Has life received a return on its investment in you? Maybe your company takes care of the needy, but what have you done for free and not because it was part of an operational plan? Do you have a sense of spirituality or joy in your life? You have a choice.

There is much you can do about what is missing. You stand at the threshold of opportunity for real change.

You may choose to calm down and be more at peace. You are running to win a race which [will end only when you step] off the track. You must start this evaluation by centering yourself. This means pausing to enjoy the subtle elements of life: a sunset, a cup of coffee, a movie with your spouse. Taking care of yourself can be a higher priority—you can take time to meditate and breathe. Trusting yourself and allowing others to connect with you will be therapeutic.

But beware. Don't make this another hard driven, list-oriented goal you must accomplish. You must relax in order to relax.

You can also reprioritize. You can put your family first and ensure uninterrupted time each day with each person. You can value "achieving" this more than you may value tangible or career-related outcomes. You can choose to parcel out time to a wider circle of friends and a greater community involvement. You can parcel out time at the office to create the vision of where you're going and steer the organization in that direction. You will accomplish more in 30 minutes of reflection at work than 4 hours of returning emails.

Finally, if you do not become more challenging of your employees, more decisive, more risk-taking, more connected with people you know less well, more empowering of others you will never have the time you need for everything else. You need to be a stronger and clearer voice in your own life. And if your voice is based on a heartfelt sense of priority and connectedness, people will follow you.

Do you think you are spending the right amounts of focus, energy, and time among the various areas of your life? Reflect on the following questions:

- As you try to achieve balance among the many roles and priorities of your life, what is working and what is not?
- What do you wish to have more of in your life? Less of?
- How has your role as a leader benefited by what you do outside work and vice versa?
- How have the priorities outside work contributed to drift at work?
- What is one thing you could do to achieve more focus and energy in your life?

Now revisit and dive a bit deeper into a topic touched on in other chapters: the costs and benefits of leading.

WEIGHING COSTS AND BENEFITS

Taking time to look at the costs and benefits of leading is important for answering the question, "Is being a leader worth the time and effort?" As you come up with responses to this question, think across all arenas of your life, including the impact it has on your extended family and friends and the networks in which you are involved in your community. See if this reflection doesn't give you further insight. Perhaps you had not recognized or articulated a particular benefit that gives you more resolve to continue your leadership journey. Perhaps you had not been able to name a specific cost but will find the language for it here.

Here is one example. Suppose you are in a global leadership role and gain pleasure from it because it lets you experience different countries and cultures. The perceived benefit here is global travel, which might include your family at times. But global travel can also entail a cost insofar as it takes you away from family or leads to bodily wear and tear. Another benefit of your global role might be that you meet colleagues across disciplines, interests, and nationalities. That expansive network may serve both your work (when you contemplate your next professional move) and your personal life (when you need to help a friend or family member find a job). Other benefits (or costs) might be financial ones. These rewards would extend beyond your work life to your personal life because they allow you to purchase goods and services such as tennis lessons, gym membership, or a new car.

Exhibit 6.1 lists many possible costs and benefits of leadership. With the list as a stimulus, make your own list of costs and benefits in your current situation. Modify or add items according to your own lights.

EXHIBIT 6.1 A SAMPLING OF COSTS AND BENEFITS OF LEADERSHIP

Costs	Benefits
Physical energy	Physical energy
Mental energy	Mental energy
Spiritual energy	Spiritual energy
Long hours at work	Pride of accomplishment
Time spent in meetings	Financial rewards
Constant obligations	Self-validation
Responsibility	Impact on people and events
Caretaking requirements of family members	Responsibility
	Service to others
Less time for nonleadership work interests	Meaning
	Attention and recognition
Visibility (being in a fishbowl)	Visibility
Public duties	Personal prominence
Isolation from peers	New connections and acquaintances
Less freedom of expression	
Pressure to produce	Helping others grow
Stress on family	Perquisites of office

(*continued*)

Costs	Benefits
Less time for family	More resources for family
Less time for other pursuits	Personal status
Emotional strains	Singular achievements
Very little feedback from boss	Heightened experience
Unhelpful feedback from boss	More autonomy
Too much travel	Travel linked to recreation
Bad relocations	Good relocations
Job insecurity	Change
	Control
	Respect
	Inclusion

Of course, the sheer number of items on either side of your column will not determine whether costs outweigh benefits or vice versa. You will need to compare the lists and assign a level of importance to each item to determine which way the scale leans. Also, examine the list in a qualitative way. What stands out for you? Write your reactions to your cost-benefit list. Overall, how do the benefits of being a leader stack up against the costs?

Does your current situation meet your needs? Or does this process further clarify why you are adrift? If the latter, are there changes in your leadership role or setting that could set you on course again? Are there changes you want to make outside work? Might it help to change how you view some aspect of the situation? Discuss this list with a friend or significant other to gain additional clarification.

FIVE STRATEGIES FOR ACHIEVING MORE BALANCE

The five strategies explored in this section can help you better focus energy and time across the various arenas of your life. All are ways to align important aspects of your life—work, family, community, health, volunteering, and learning.

In *What Happy Women Know* (2008), Dan Baker, Cathy Greenberg, and Ina Yalof advise: "Clearly, there is no one right way to combine work and family life, only the way that's right for you. Ask yourself which combination does the best job of meeting most of your needs" (p. 146). Ellen Kossek and Brenda Lautsch (2008) reflect the same view with their notion of "flexstyles." You have to find your unique approach to managing the flexibility between work and life to help them fit better together.

We believe this is about finding within yourself your center of gravity—a holistic place where things come together, where the world is right for you now. This insight can emerge from a combination of your competencies, values, relationships, and experiences. It's also an insight you need to revisit and reconsider regularly as changes call for future adjustments.

Start by asking, "What isn't working, or what is missing in my life?" One executive we worked with said she was missing structure and organization (specifically in her client files). With many clients to manage, she was losing track of things that needed her attention. We set up an electronic update sheet for her to update electronic client records. The sheet has made updates routine, a single change she credits with reducing her overall stress.

Reflect on the following areas of your life: career, family, self, community, and spirituality. What is missing? What isn't working? Then use these tactics (and others) as starting points for ways to achieve more balance:

- *Integrate*. Identify what you want and create a life space to accommodate it.
- *Narrow*. Choose what's important, and eliminate the nonessential.
- *Moderate*. Set limits on the time and energy you give to tasks and roles.
- *Sequence*. Set priorities. Don't do everything at once.
- *Add resources*. Get the people, systems, and money you need to take the pressure off you.

You may find that using one tactic is all you need. Alternatively, you may find that a combination of tactics works best. As you will see, each has many variations.

Integrating

Integration is perhaps the most comprehensive approach to achieving relative balance. Its premise is that different needs and activities of your life can be interwoven into a synergistic whole. The idea is to identify what you really want in each area of your life and then design a life space in which you can accomplish your goals in an integrated way.

The antithesis of integration is partitioning, or creating or maintaining artificial barriers between areas of life. One person described trying to compartmentalize and the frustrating results that ensued:

> What I tend to do is try to order my life—very, very structured. At 10:05 it's time to hug the wife. I find myself giving up spontaneity, trying to juggle conflicting needs. I get pretty creative: "Well, if I do this, if I schedule this meeting here and I rush over, and everything is right and I hit all the lights, then I can be at the dance recital." And so there's always tension and stress.

Integrating might initially sound like the opposite of balancing, since balance is often viewed as drawing lines among work, family, and personal life. When you begin to integrate, the lines become blurred. In our view, the blurring can be helpful for balance. Rigidly compartmentalizing is often counterproductive. Integration can help ease boundaries that you set. For example, you can work at home with your family nearby instead of at the office. Bring the kids to work one day. Make personal phone calls at work during lunch hour, or combine paid work trips with personal vacations. Other ideas include doing community service with your family, asking your family to join you on your morning run, or sitting by a pool while you work.

Employees and employers are now knocking down these false barriers. Boundaries can be flexible, and one can choose when to overlap. It may make sense to bring your family along on a business trip and take small excursions in your free time. We know of some women who travel with a small child and a caregiver so that they can have evenings with the child and not agonize about being away.

Of course, integration is not without problems. In trying to meet two needs with one solution, we may not meet both or even either to anyone's satisfaction. Bringing a child on a business trip may work better for a parent who works outside the home than for a child accustomed to receiving a parent's undivided attention during the day.

Consider these questions as you reflect on using an integrating strategy:

- Which boundaries would you like to soften or blend?
- Where do you partition your life?
- What types of integration have you already tried, and what have been the results?
- Are there any areas of your life that could become more integrated?
- How might this contribute to your life satisfaction?
- How might both sides be given more benefit?

Narrowing

We can do only so much at any point in time. Who among us doesn't know someone who is trying to do too much or who has felt overwhelmed by all those top-level commitments we view as nonnegotiable? Narrowing the range of what's important may be the key to better balance.

Narrowing means deciding to offload a bunch of tasks, goals, relationships, and expectations. We all need to clean our mental closets once in a while. We do this most often at major transitions (for example, key birthdays, relocations, promotions) and at times of serious difficulty (for example, severe criticism or failure, family trouble, illness). The commitments that survive the cleaning then become more important, more manageable, and easier to integrate.

Narrowing can happen at deeper levels too. Some people stay single partly so that they can devote more of their life to their work. Some marry but elect not to have children. In many marriages, one partner forgoes personal ambitions and a full-time career so that the other partner can take on bigger work challenges.

Choices can be made in other areas as well. It may be important to attend religious services, but that doesn't mean you have to accept a lay leadership position. Perhaps it's ideal to get to the gym five times a week, but a treadmill workout at home two or three times a week may have to do. A promotion to vice president of international sales might be nice, but it may not fit with everything else that's going on in your life.

One executive explained to us how he has managed to narrow his commitments: "I've tried to cut down on a lot of things in my life, try to spend time on the things that are most important to me, and consciously try to say, 'Well, gee, is that really that big a deal?' If it's not, I just say no, refuse to do it, and that allows me to have enough time to do the things that are most important to me."

The narrowing strategy focuses on making only commitments that you can keep. Doing things well may be more important than taking on work that pushes you to your limits.

As you think about narrowing, consider these questions:

- What are your most important commitments?
- What commitments do you maintain beyond their real degree of importance to you?
- Which of your tasks, goals, relationships, and expectations, and those of others in your purview, can you set aside or even discard?
- Where can you commit more fully by spreading yourself over fewer tasks?

Moderating

Moderating expectations is another way of honoring commitments, especially when you can't drop any of them. "Everything in moderation" in this case means spending the right amount of time in each area of life, not looking for perfection. Must the report be perfect? Must your child's birthday party have clowns and storytellers?? Must you take the lead on every project?

The same executive we quoted previously about narrowing had this to say about moderating:

> I have an agreement with my wife that I will not work later than 6:00 in the evening, and I live by that 99.9 percent of the time. I do come in [to work] early in the morning, but we're OK with that because it doesn't take away from the family. As early as I get out, I usually go to bed fairly early. But I seldom take work home. When I have a project I need to work on over the weekend—which is very, very rare—I'll come in the office early Saturday or Sunday and plug away and get home midmorning or by lunch time. Then the rest of the day is committed to the family. I think that has had a tremendous effect on the home life.

Some people unfortunately assume that those who seem to balance work and nonwork activities successfully are not fully committed, dedicated members of the corporate team—and perhaps they are even freeloaders who are milking more from the organization than they are giving back. But as you now know from research we have cited, managers and leaders who maintain good roles outside work often perform better on the job than those who maniacally work, work, work.

We suggest that you identify and invest in the specific combination of roles that enhances your psychological well-being, self-awareness, and work effectiveness. And as you invest in these roles, don't assume that you have to fulfill every one at the same level. Think about what is good enough.

As you reflect on moderating, consider these questions:

- Do you have too many salient commitments?
- Can you scale back on the time you devote to each?
- Are your or others' expectations about you too high in some areas right now?
- What might be more realistic?

- How might you change your expectations of all that has to be accomplished?

Sequencing

This strategy says, "Yes, you can have it all [or almost all], but not all at once!" Sequencing doesn't mean entirely giving up on options but rather deciding which things to do first. One executive we talked with takes a seasonal perspective: "I've always said that September and October are bad family months because I'm so busy at work. November and December are great family months because I'm not so busy at work. So the family understands what's going on."

If you take a proactive approach to planning how you will attend to your priorities across weeks and months, you will recognize that not everything has to be done at once. However, sequencing carries some risks. Putting something off until later may mean you'll never get to it. It may be superseded by a new stream of high priorities, illness, or something else. It's also possible that what looks so important today will look less so later on.

Many organizations start each year's budget discussion with a long wish list of new ventures, capital projects, staffing additions, and other desired goals. As they get down to discussing strategy and reality, the list gets a lot shorter (a narrowing strategy). Then the priorities that are left can be sequenced throughout the year so that limited resources can be applied at the right time.

As you turn to the role of sequencing in your life, reflecting on these questions will point you in the right direction:

- What work and personal goals would you put on your list of top priorities?
- Which few goals really require the most thought and effort now, ahead of all the others?
- In what order would you tackle these priorities?
- Which ones must be done first in order to be able to accomplish the others?

- What will be the benefits to you and others from sequencing these tasks?

Adding Resources

If the commitments are important and can't realistically be dropped, moderated, or postponed, add resources—for example:

- Get a bigger budget.
- Add staff—permanent or temporary, perfect or otherwise—at work.
- Align with people who have what you need.
- Share resources with colleagues.
- Get rid of impediments and obstacles.
- Free up underused resources.
- Hire others to assist with personal tasks: cleaning the house, babysitting, mowing the lawn, and so on.

If some of these are unavailable, look to others. If times are lean, think about trading services or resources rather than buying. This might not only help you free up your own time but also provide benefits to others. The real question is how you use resources to help you in all areas and not just to do a better job at work:

- What additional resources could relieve your stress or help you accomplish your work faster? Where would you apply them, and why?
- Which resources in the list above have you used recently? Did they work?
- What other means could you use to improve how you juggle your multiple priorities?

We know that using the right strategies to deal with the conflicts and tensions of a busy life is no easy task. Circumstances are constantly changing, and thus adjustments will need to be made on a regular basis. In order to increase your effectiveness as a leader, continue to try different strategies to find the right combination or recipe that works for you.

CONCLUSION

This chapter drew connections between the worlds of work and personal life. It also looked at five basic strategies for achieving balance: integrating, narrowing, moderating, sequencing, and adding resources. We hope these strategies help you better manage the work of leadership, get you out of drift, or even help you to take on more leadership in your life.

Think about your responses to the questions posed throughout this chapter. Now reflect on the following questions to see what else you might uncover about reducing the stress that comes as you seek to balance work and personal life:

- How would you fully describe your own tensions and conflicts of balance?
- If you were able to lead your life in an ideal way, what would it look like?
- What assumptions are preventing you from making progress?
- Who do you know who has found a way to manage balance effectively? What could that person share that might help you?
- What tactics will you try? Is there anything standing in the way of starting to use these tactics today or tomorrow?

The final chapter of this book will help you synthesize and consolidate your work from earlier chapters in the book. It will also help you consider the implications for future decisions you make as a leader.

CHAPTER SEVEN

THE LEADER IN YOU

Discovering the leader in you is an ongoing process, not a one-time, isolated event. After working through the first six chapters, you have probably accumulated many insights about yourself, your challenges, and your opportunities as leader. This final chapter helps you develop a clearer picture of yourself as a leader now and in the future. It outlines a process that begins with mapping information on the leadership framework by which Chapters Two through Six were organized. You'll begin with brief phrases that you'll subsequently expand and eventually incorporate into holistic statements of purpose and, finally, a letter to yourself.

This chapter also presents a process you can use to work through any major impending decision you face in considering a larger leadership role. Furthermore, you'll gain some advice on how to enhance, support, and extend your discovery process of why, when, where, and how you may lead.

USING THE DISCOVERING LEADERSHIP FRAMEWORK

Let's return to the Discovering Leadership Framework we introduced in Chapter One (Figure 1.1). This framework helps you assess the context in which you lead, analyze your specific leadership dilemmas, and identify specific themes and patterns that have an impact on your effectiveness as a leader. Figure 7.1 uses the framework to highlight the

147

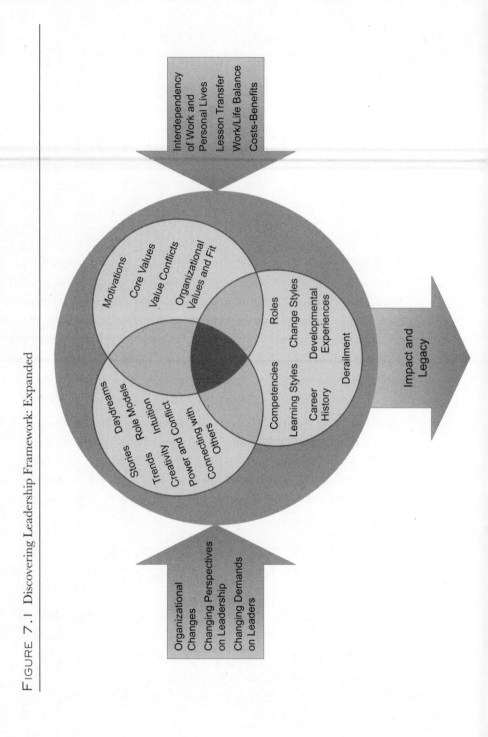

FIGURE 7.1 Discovering Leadership Framework: Expanded

key concepts from each chapter as a reminder of what was discussed. We hope these key concepts will remind you of your thoughts as you read each chapter.

So that you can use the framework to capture salient ideas, thoughts, and insights about yourself and your situation, we've posted a blank version at www.josseybass.com/go/discoveringtheleaderinyou. If you are not able to download the blank copy, sketch the framework on a sheet of paper, and fill it in as you work your way through this chapter. To help you get oriented, Figure 7.2 illustrates an example of a leader who shared with us how he used the framework to guide his leader discovery process.

Take a few minutes now to write the most pertinent words or phrases in each section of the blank version you downloaded or sketched for yourself. For example, in the organizational realities section, you might list the key issues in your organization. List those things that are affecting your leadership the most, such as the key technological trends, the financial health of your organization, factors related to a pending merger that is threatening leadership jobs, growth pressures on your organization, notes about your boss's recently vacated position (which you might consider taking), or other contextual issues.

Similarly, in the section on vision, focus on the role that leadership plays in your life, and include phrases describing your leadership vision. As you fill in each section, refer to Figure 7.1 for key topics or revisit the previous chapters to bring back ideas that came to you as you read each one. Your responses to the questions at the end of each chapter should help you as well.

Next, step back and reflect on what you've written. What connections do you see between various thoughts within each section and between one section and another? For example, do you see a connection between your main view of leadership (Chapter Two) and your leadership competencies (Chapter Five)? How do your core values (Chapter Four) relate to your ideas and choices about role models (Chapter Three)?

Look for leadership themes in your initial reflections. Suppose your view of leadership and your motivation for leading are related to service and you picked "nurturer" and "facilitator" as preferred leadership roles.

FIGURE 7.2 Discovering Leadership Framework: Example

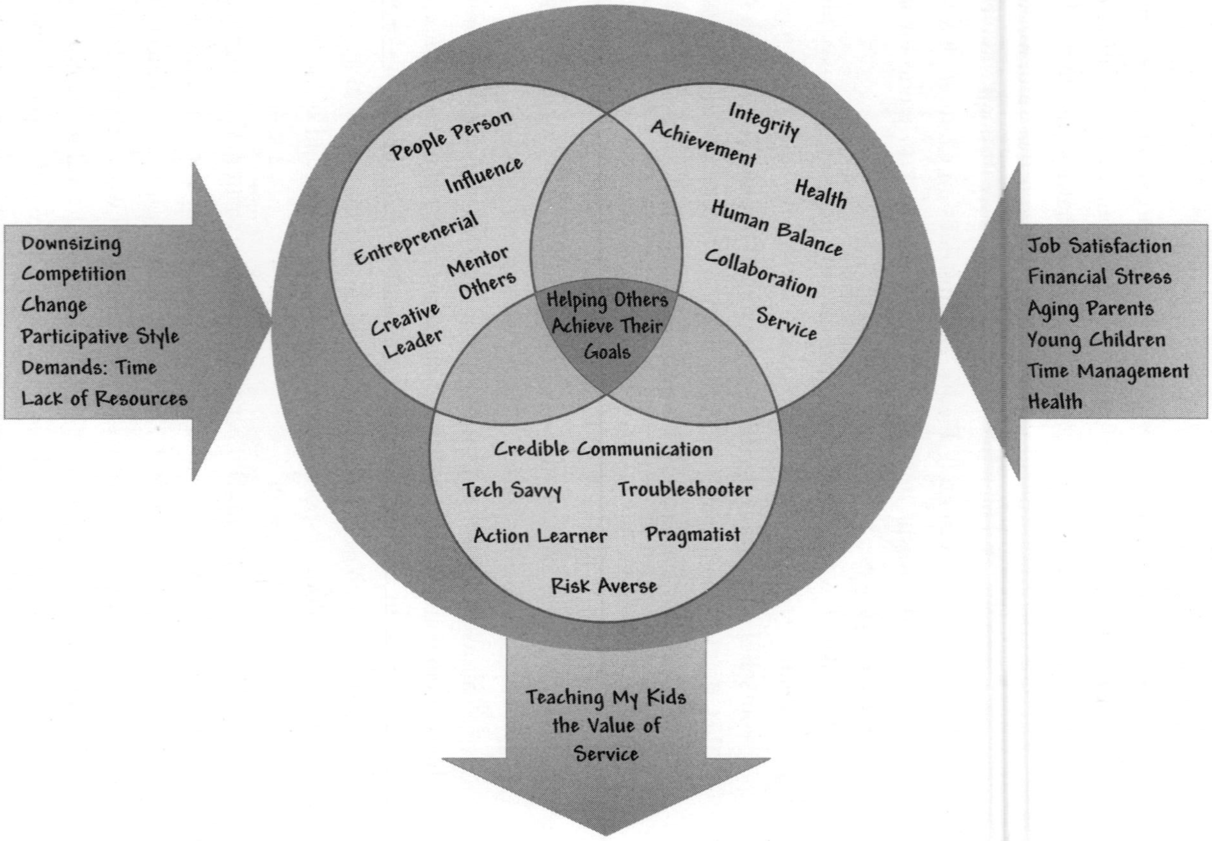

From that you might distill a leadership theme of "giving to others." Or suppose that getting things done through others is one of your strong competencies, that you favor the role of coach, that one of your core values is diverse perspectives, and that your vision incorporates a desire to lead in a global context. From that pattern, you might cull a theme of "global leader who maximizes the potential of a diverse workforce."

Now step back further to see if a picture emerges from your framework as whole. Do you like what you see? Does it align with your current leadership role or with a different role you might be seeking? What core issue needs attention? Does this picture describe the impact you wish to have?

Did you write much more in some sections than in others? Are some pieces missing? If so, access another blank framework, and create the portrait of your ideal future. Pick a future point in time (say, three years from now), and press yourself to write in each section. Do you expect the organizational context around you to have changed a great deal? Write a phrase to capture that future context. Do you envision significantly different leadership roles? Write them down even if there is no guarantee that they will be available to you. What competencies—old and new—will need to be in your leadership profile? And so on for all five sections. What implications can you draw from this future version of the framework for your development as a leader?

IDENTIFYING YOUR LEADERSHIP PURPOSE

In this part of the chapter, you will use the work you carried out in the framework's sections to generate new key statements about yourself as a leader. We challenge you to come up with five or six. From these statements, you can further define how leadership fits in your life.

Here are some key signature lines written by senior leaders who have worked with us:

- "I prefer building a team and seeing what we can accomplish together."

- "I just can't sit back when there is leadership work to be done. I find it rewarding to fix things."
- "I need my privacy. If leadership means living in a fishbowl all of the time, then I don't think I am interested."
- "What turns me on is winning. I love it when we beat the competition or end up high in our industry's rankings."
- "I can't take on a larger leadership role at this time. My plate is full between work and family responsibilities. I am comfortable staying in an individual contributor role."
- "I am at my best when I coach others. I would like to help the organization more by building the next generation of talent."
- "I get energized by helping people solve their problems."

In writing your own five or six statements, do you see any additional themes? What self-revelations or self-confirmations do the themes suggest? Self-revelations are new insights that arise from this discovery process. Self-confirmations identify core capabilities or values that you already knew but now can hold with more clarity and conviction. Test each of your key themes for insights.

A service-minded leader's confirmation might be, "I won't be totally satisfied in a leadership role unless I am in a servant leadership role." For a leader whose vision includes a global component, a revelatory statement might be, "I need to find a leadership role with opportunities to lead a globally diverse team to deliver a socially responsible product or service." Although this exercise won't always result in a major eye-opening revelation, often you will come up with an insight that has been right under your nose.

Each statement tries to say, in essence, "Here's where I stand. This really matters to me. The place that other things find in my life will depend on their fit with this." You'll know when you've hit on an authentic statement when you share it with your spouse, your parents, or your best friends, and they confirm it reflects the real you. The statements you write will move you closer to a central statement of purpose.

Now look at Figure 7.3. At the intersection of *vision*, *values*, and *profile* appears the word *purpose*. Reflect on your leadership vision, your core

FIGURE 7.3 Discovering Leadership Framework: Purpose

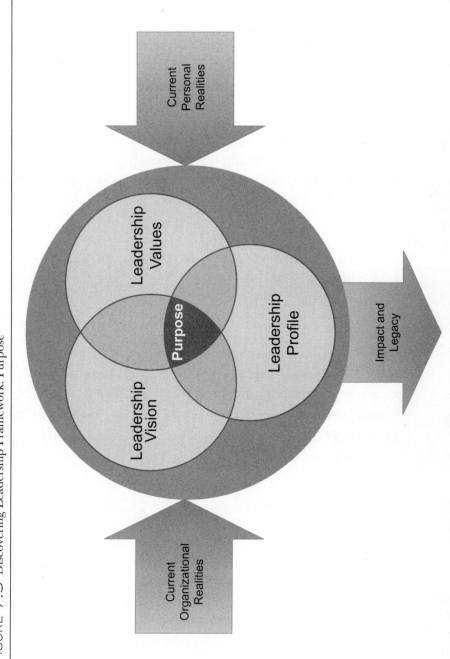

values, and your signature strengths (where you really excel), and try to write a sentence or two about your leadership purpose. As a leader, what do you really want to accomplish? What is so important to you that you are determined to make it happen? Refer back to Figure 7.2 to see the overall purpose as written by one senior executive. Here are some examples:

- "I want to start a new program for underprivileged children."
- "I want to develop the talent capacity in our organization to meet the challenges we face in the next three to five years in a way that we are perceived as best-in-class."
- "I want to become president of my division in order to have the influence and impact I envision."
- "I want to lead the corporate philanthropy efforts in our organization."

As you reflect on your purpose statement, consider closely the impact and legacy parts of the framework. Your overall leadership purpose, when accomplished, will be the impact you have and often the legacy you leave. Don't rush through this part. Take time to reflect, and imagine yourself making the kind of difference you want to make. Does your purpose lead to the impact you wish to have? What do you hope others will say about your leadership?

WRITE A LETTER TO YOURSELF

Now that you've filled in the framework (both current and future), articulated some key statements about your leadership, written an initial statement about your leadership purpose, and reflected on your leadership legacy, let's use another process for describing the future.

For this process, we'd like you to write yourself a letter. We have found that when people use different methods in their discovery process, they produce higher-quality insights than when they use only a single approach. By completing the framework, you captured the essence of who you are and came to better understand the context in which you lead. By completing the future framework, you outlined what you imagine the future to be in each of the sections of the framework. A letter affords you an opportunity to create a picture. In the letter, you can use your creativity to express more fully your hopes and desires related to the leader in you, particularly the future leader.

The letter-writing activity will feel different from filling out the framework. In many ways, the letter addresses the gap between your current and future state. What are the important steps you need to take to move from your current framework to your future framework? How might you turn these steps into goals? What do you want to continue doing as a leader, and what new things do you want to incorporate?

We're giving you only two rules for your letter: express your future in terms of clear goals, and name some people you will need to help you achieve your goals. The rest is up to you. Address your letter to yourself, sign it however you like, organize it however you want, and use whatever style of writing you like (a poem, a story, an essay, a correspondence, a journal entry—any style is all right as long as it's comfortable for you). Expand on what you have learned about yourself, push those insights even further, and try to create a compelling, descriptive picture of the future.

Throughout this book, we have included letters or portions of them that senior executives have written during their experience with CCL's Leadership at the Peak program. This is your chance to participate in this powerful activity. Go back and reread some of them (they are all italicized to help you find them easily), or read the letter that follows as an example of what you might write. Your letter can look completely different and can also address different issues. Just use the examples to get you started. Whatever you write, you can always go back and revise it—but don't think so much about that. Have some fun with this activity; let your thoughts flow, and see where you end up.

Dear—

After spending an entire week of introspective thought, I have concluded that there are some things in life that require action. If I am successful in working at these things, I believe it will be beneficial not only to myself, but also to those around me; whether these people are coworkers, family, friends, or new acquaintances.

First, I have learned that my peers at work have a much lower image of me and my capabilities that I ever imagined. I believe I can do a better job of getting connected to them. I will make every effort to gather more emotional input from them before making a decision or striking a position.

Second, I intend to be more productive in giving feedback to my employees on a regular basis. My initial tendency is to operate like a solo pilot in my daily activities. I need to fix this problem because as I advance in my career, the ability to interact with people and provide constructive and critical feedback to help them develop will be essential.

Third, I realize that life is finite. I need to be more aware of my physical and mental well-being as I approach the next decade. I intend to pay more attention to what I put into my mouth and become more selfish about getting adequate sleep and exercise. I will feel better about myself, and that will make me a better person at home and in the office.

Fourth, I intend to address an issue with my parents about being more active in my children's lives. I need to do this because it is a source of stress for me and my family.

Share your letter with individuals you are confident can help you. Make some commitments to them so that they can hold you accountable for achieving your goals and working toward this future picture.

THE LEADERSHIP DECISION LADDER

We have said that discovering who you are as a leader is an ongoing process for making the right choices and recalibrating your choices as those challenges change or as you reframe them. From day to day or week to week, your increased self-awareness helps you stay on track and keeps you from drifting. But what about the moment when a decision has to be made? What do you do at the point you are offered your first managerial opportunity or you take a leap into a larger leader role? How should you proceed to make a choice? Consider one story.

Reuben Daniels faced a big decision. He had traveled a predictable yet demanding path through college, graduate school, and early employment as he became a highly qualified clinical scientist. As a more and more accomplished clinical researcher (with both an M.D. and a Ph.D.), with a focus on molecular medicine, he loved doing research and being part of a collaborative lab team. By his late thirties, he had been promoted from senior research scientist to the director of advanced research at the institute where he worked. The institute was affiliated with a university's hospital and medical and other graduate schools. As the director of advanced research, he managed and mentored twelve younger scientists.

Because of his success in the lab, Reuben was named as one of three vice presidents on the institute's executive team. As a result, the scope of his supervision expanded from the 12 scientists in his lab to include about a third of the institute's 210 employees. This enterprise-wide role proved to be gratifying in some ways: Reuben could now set policy direction for a number of units and build a strong cadre of high-potential scientists. But the role also proved irritating: he spent much less time in the lab doing science and much more time in meetings talking about science. Responding to e-mails also took time. In one instance, he became embroiled in administrative conflict around the lack of lab space and the need to bring in more outside funding to support the institute's increasingly lean scientific infrastructure. At the end of most days, Reuben thought the trade-offs he had made between science and administration were worth it, but he wasn't at all sure he wanted any further advancement. This was as far from his beloved lab as he wanted to go.

Two years later, Reuben's boss resigned abruptly to take a position elsewhere. The executive vice president for health affairs called Reuben to her office and asked him to take over as president of the institute. The other two vice presidents would not be candidates; one's health was poor, and the other was clearly in over his head. The job was Reuben's to take or to refuse.

Reuben requested a week to consider. As it happened, he had participated in a week-long leadership development course that included spending time with an executive coach a year earlier. He had done his homework, so to speak, on his values, his life balance issues, and his personal long-term vision. That experience had confirmed his commitment to limit his organizational advancement so he could stay close enough to his research projects and keep up his personal and family life. But now this!

Reuben still had his coach's phone number, and the coach was ready to help. They had long discussions by phone and e-mail about what was important, what Rueben's leadership agenda might be, and how he could best contribute to science and society. How would the president's job affect his ability to stay on top of emerging events in his scientific field? How could he be president of a prestigious institute when he didn't do well as a public speaker and couldn't even keep his own desk in order? Could he handle the politics that sparked the former president's departure? Would he be able to bring in big money or make the staff cuts necessary to align costs with grant revenues? After a week of reflection, Reuben decided to take the job because it would be the capstone challenge of his life. He negotiated executive support for the research agenda he wished to pursue. Since then, and so far, he is doing quite well.

The point of this story is that Reuben assumed the new opportunity by choice, not by default. His decision process included a serious analysis of what looked right for him. He used the knowledge he had about the context in which he would lead, the leadership demands, and his own interests and abilities. He also found a coach—a sounding board—to help him sort out the issues. In the end, he determined that leading the institute fit his future picture and that he was willing to accept the trade-offs.

Rung by Rung

The leadership decision ladder in Figure 7.4 can help you sort out a large decision in a way similar to what Reuben encountered. A ladder is

FIGURE 7.4 Leadership Decision Ladder

an obvious metaphor for a sequence of steps, and in this case it signifies the stages you climb as you decide whether to take on a leadership role. The ladder embodies the same or similar questions as those in the Discovering Leadership Framework, but it presents a different perspective and a different order to the questions. Such small changes can present new insights. Consider that:

- Wherever you are on a ladder, there is potentially another step to take.
- When you look down at previous rungs, you are reminded of choices you made in getting to the rung on which you now stand.
- Your vantage point and view of the surroundings (the context surrounding your leadership) are slightly different at each step on the ladder.

The ladder has five rungs, each representing a point of connection between leadership choices you have made in the past and the context surrounding those choices. In thinking about how you relate to this ladder, you may find that you are moving up the ladder toward more leadership responsibility in a relatively concerted way or that you have paused on one of the rungs as you postpone further leadership commitments. You might conclude that the view you have from the rung you're on is just right; staying where you are provides you with what you need at a particular point in time.

Of course, it's not realistic to think that your leadership capacity is defined along just one set of rails and rungs. Other leadership ladders appear in other situations and times in life, at work or at home, in your community, or in unfamiliar places. You can also always step down from one leadership ladder to climb another that appeals to you more. You can move up and down any leadership ladder as you need to revisit decisions and accomplishments, recall the perspective from lower down, remind yourself of the stages you've gone through and choices you made to get to your current position, or simply recheck the sturdiness of those lower rungs as they support all the rungs above. No matter what leadership ladder you're on, your ultimate goal is to make decisions from the highest rung, where you have the best view of all the circumstances that you currently face. Here is what each rung represents in the decision to lead:

•   *Rung 1: Grounding yourself.* This rung represents basic self-knowledge about your personal vision, values, and competencies. At your core, who are you, and how do these core factors affect you as a leader? Throughout your career and life, you will stand again on this first rung, updating your self-knowledge, reevaluating it each time you assess whether a new opportunity is worth pursuing. Occasionally standing on the first rung is a good way to reconfirm your purpose as a human and the authenticity of your leadership journey.

•   *Rung 2: Developing a vision.* What is your vision for leadership? What do you want to accomplish, and how will being a leader help you? Do you have something more to offer the world: a skill, a message, or even a different reality? Is there some specific impact you want to make? This could be your overall purpose as a leader, and it serves as a basis for where you want to go with leadership. Looking down at the work you did on rung 1, think in personal terms about what you have to say or want to express about yourself as a leader. How will a new opportunity to lead help you accomplish your ultimate purpose in life? Many people's purpose becomes cloudy and hard to define as new variables come into play. Periodically stand on this second rung to reassess how your purpose can help you strengthen the connections between who you are as a leader and what you want to do in that role.

- *Rung 3: Engaging challenges.* This rung is where curiosity, adventure, and challenge come into play. What new things about leadership would you like to learn or try? What might be missing from your repertoire that you'll need in a new leadership position or opportunity? Will a new leadership opportunity provide or allow you the growth, learning, and experimentation that you'll need to improve your skills? At this rung, you need to confront whether you're willing to take on a new challenge; don't assume the answer is always yes.

- *Rung 4: Accounting for others.* At some point in a leader's journey, you realize that your effectiveness is closely tied to the efforts of other people. One executive in his mid-forties recently told us that he finally figured that his success going forward will be a function of how well he works with and through others versus what he is able to accomplish through his own efforts. What do you want to accomplish for and with others or for an organization? If you seize a leadership opportunity, what larger goals will be advanced or fulfilled? How will others benefit from your leadership, and how can they help achieve the changes you desire? Is what you hope to accomplish for and with others realistic? Have you checked to see that the support, resources, job responsibility, and context will work together with your insights to make your hopes for them a reality?

- *Rung 5: Picking your time.* Is this the right time for you to take on a new or expanded opportunity? Is your personal context compatible with anticipated demands such as the scope of the work or the amount of travel it requires? Do you have your family's support? What will be the benefits and trade-offs of this role for people close to you? Will it require a move or changes for others? Will this leadership opportunity open another opportunity that you think you want? If so, is this the step that will take you and the people important to you further? Will saying yes or no now limit your chances or options later?

Before You Step Up to the Next Rung

At the end of the day, each step of the leader ladder requires making concrete decisions. We have some suggestions for you to consider as you move through the decision process:

- *Sleep on it.* Let your insights marinate before making any final conclusions or public pronouncements. Your conclusions may look different after reflection.
- *Share it.* Share your thoughts with friends you trust to be sounding boards and providing honest feedback to you. Confirmation about your discoveries and your plans is welcome. Disconfirming feedback is equally important.
- *Experiment.* Before making any big moves based on your current thinking, try experimenting. Try out some new behaviors. Float an idea past your boss. Volunteer. You don't have to make permanent choices or decisions before you test out your hunches about leading. For example, if you want to think more positively about the situation you find yourself in, try it. Or if you find yourself underchallenged, volunteer to think about another group's current business challenge, and offer advice. Let your experiments inform your thinking.

CONTINUING TO DISCOVER THE LEADER IN YOU

This chapter (and this book, overall) should have already helped you draw new insights into your journey and development as a leader. Perhaps you are redefining where and how you want to lead. You may decide right now that you are ready to take on a leadership role or advance into a larger one. Or maybe you want to continue with self-discovery and see how you can maximize your development in place. Perhaps you don't want a new role; you just want to keep from getting stale or bored in the one you have.

Wherever you are right now, we think it's worth taking a little more time to clarify (or further clarify) your goals and tap into your social network for advice and support.

Clarifying Goals

In the letter to yourself, you outlined some important goals. We assume you already know a lot about setting goals and techniques for making them specific and measurable. You also know that to set yourself up for success in achieving your goals, you must begin to articulate the details of an action plan. The action plan must have deadlines, the resources you will need to accomplish your goals, ideas for overcoming obstacles, and a list of benefits you will accrue. To help confirm that you are targeting the right goals and that they are clear, consider these questions:

- How has this discovery process helped you be more certain about your role as a leader? Where do you still have uncertainty? What else do you need to help you?
- Do you still see yourself drifting? Do you want to tackle the problem of drift? If so, what tactics will you use to get out of drift?
- Do you identify more now with yourself as a leader? Do you imagine taking small moments to exercise leadership as well as pursuing additional formal roles of leadership?
- What other information do you need to help you clarify what you've discovered about the leader in you?
- Are you stuck on a particular rung of your leadership decision ladder? From whom do you need more help to get unstuck?

Wherever you see a gap, unfinished work, or an unreached desire, this is another place where you need to set goals. Also, don't forget to think in concrete terms about how accomplishing these goals will help you in your journey as a leader and how you will measure your success. You don't need to do all this on your own; in fact, it's important to seek the advice and assistance of others.

Getting the Help You Need

You gain little or nothing from making this journey toward greater leadership alone. There are many ways to get help; one of them is through formal and informal feedback from other people. It's rare to get the opportunity to see yourself as others see you. Honest feedback from members of your network can help you confirm that the goals you have set for yourself are the right ones. Feedback can help you know how the changes you seek for yourself may come across as beneficial or disruptive to other members of your organization and even to your family and friends. Feedback can also help you evaluate setbacks or opportunities.

Because taking a leadership position often means trading away honest feedback (the higher your position, the likelier that people will tell you what they think you want to hear rather than what you need to hear), you will have to work hard to provide an environment in which people feel safe to give you the feedback you need. One place to look for that kind of feedback is in the safety of your developmental relationships (with coaches, mentors, and role models).

There is no prototypical developmental relationship, and there is no single role or combination of roles required to make a relationship developmental. Since that's the case, we urge you to seek out multiple relationships that can fuel your development. Figure out what you need developmentally, and then consider who can best help you fill that need. Embrace those around you who will give you honest feedback. At CCL, we encourage feedback that is totally kind and totally honest. If you can find people who give you that kind of feedback, consider it a huge gift. The key is to match the right relationship to the right need. For example, if you think you want the next formal leadership role above you, talk with people who hold or have held that position. Ask them about the strategic priorities in the role, its demands, what they like and dislike about it. Of course, if this person is your boss and may feel threatened, be savvy about finding someone comparable who does feel comfortable sharing his or her point of view.

Seek out skeptics so that you are forced to consider all possible perspectives on the decision. A developmental relationship with someone who thinks very differently than you do can be of great benefit, especially if you value his or her point of view. Or consider working with someone who is good at a particular competency that is still a stretch for you. For example, individuals often get promoted into a leadership role because they are excellent doers. They get the job done and do it well. However, they don't always know much about getting work done through others and developing other people. If that were your situation, you would want to seek out someone who is particularly good at spotting talent, setting development plans, and giving targeted developmental feedback.

Developmental relationships need not be long term or intense. What you're looking for is simply a different perspective, for example, or new knowledge, a willingness to engage with your ideas, a measurement of your capabilities, or just a good listener who keeps you motivated. Lateral, subordinate, and even relationships outside work can all be developmental. An experienced colleague, a peer in another division, or even the retired executive who lives down the street may be a good match.

Cynthia McCauley and Christina Douglas (2004) identify different types of developmental relationships. Here are five that might particularly suit your leadership discovery process.

Sounding Board

This is a colleague or group of people with whom you can discuss your satisfactions and dissatisfactions about your leadership role. As a sounding board, the person might simply listen as you think aloud about vision, values, self-awareness, and other aspects of your leadership; or it might be someone to whom you can pose specific questions, like, "I believe I act in tune with my values, but what have you noticed about my actions that might tell a different story?" or "Do I come across as unmotivated? What gives you that impression?"

A sounding board should be someone you see on a regular basis and is willing to listen to you carefully. Look for someone who is good at thinking out loud and considering alternatives, and a person you can trust to understand and appreciate your uncertainties.

Counselor

A counselor encourages you to explore the emotional aspects of your work. He or she can, without judging, let you vent and express your frustrations and negative emotions. For instance, perhaps you doubt your capacity to develop and sustain a leadership vision because that kind of thinking has always made you uncomfortable—you have always left the pie-in-the-sky thinking to others. But as a leader, people expect you to express a vision, and they want to know that you have one. Now you must deal with your impatience about something that you have previously regarded as impractical, unnecessary, or even nonsensical.

A counselor can help you take a different perspective so that you can adapt and develop a capacity you previously ignored. For this role, choose someone you can trust as a confidant—someone who is empathetic and objective but also clearheaded enough to see through the excuses you make and call you out for procrastinating.

Cheerleader

This supporting role provides valuable encouragement and affirmation. Seek out someone who can express confidence and affirm and celebrate your accomplishments. Such a person might take you out to dinner to celebrate a milestone, or join you on a fishing trip or some other excursion when you choose your leadership opportunity. When looking for a cheerleader, ask yourself who around you always makes you feel competent. Look for someone you can share your small successes with or someone in a position to reward your accomplishments.

Companion

Where would Lewis be without Clark? And where would their Corps of Discovery have ended up without Sacagawea, a native Shoshone, accompanying the group as a knowledgeable companion? In terms of discovering the leader in you, *companion* refers to someone who can accompany you on the journey. If you know someone else who is engaged in self-discovery as a leader, consider asking him or her to share experiences with you. Each of you can discuss such things as your respective development progress, how each of you arrived at this stage in your development, and where each of you plans to go from here. This kind of relationship will make each of you stronger and more resolved as you share stories of struggle and success, knowing you're not in this alone. Do you know a colleague who faced a similar situation? If so, talk to that person.

Mentor

Some organizations formalize and extend mentoring over a period of time. But even in the absence of such a program, there may be a more senior leader in your organization who has already been through a process similar to the one that you are now undergoing and is willing to mentor you. He or she can provide an organizational perspective, linking your developmental quest to issues of talent development, business strategies, and personnel practices. You might find a mentor outside your organization who has had experiences like your own and is particularly interested in helping you define yourself as a leader. When considering someone to become your mentor, be sure to discuss together whether he or she has the time, motivation, and experience to help.

Staying on Track

So far in your journey through this book, you have come to some concrete decisions about how leadership fits in your life. You have set some goals, you have thought about the help you need to reach these goals, and now we need to make sure you have an ongoing process to support you throughout your leadership journey. It is important to constantly assess how you are doing in your journey as a leader. Are you on track? Should you step down a rung or two to revisit key dimensions of your leadership? Which performance indicators should you track?

Being a leader requires taking a lifelong perspective on learning, growth, and development. Your goals will undoubtedly change over time, and thus monitoring progress against your goals also needs to be ongoing. There are five key overarching steps in the monitoring process (Hannum and Hoole, 2009):

1. Articulate development goals in behaviorally measurable terms.
2. Develop a plan with specific actions and dates for deliverables.
3. Measure your progress through systematic collection of data using a variety of data collection tools.
4. Identify barriers and resources to help you overcome your barriers.
5. Revisit and revise your action plan as conditions change.

It is this last step that is often missed and causes individuals to drift. When conditions change, individuals don't take stock of the impact.

Leaders have many specific methods for evaluating their progress, from measures of organizational performance to formal assessments such as multirater feedback on their performance to seeking informal feedback from colleagues. What's important is developing a systematic monitoring and evaluation plan so that you have data, qualitative or quantitative, to help you understand what is going well or not so well. With data, you will be in a good position to make midcourse corrections.

CONCLUSION

Discovering the leader in you often blends difficult lessons and astonishing serendipity. There is no single path toward choosing a leadership that is right for you and for the people with whom you work. There is no one starting point, no finish line, no starting gun except the one you fire yourself. Successful leadership is a lifelong task of perpetual self-examination. During the process of self-discovery, concepts merge and shift as ideas about one issue spark ideas about others. Rewards and tasks change in relation to their contexts, and your own goals change over time. Each change demands a different mix of a leader's resources. You will always experience moments of drift or uncertainty. Our hope is that in those moments when you find yourself drifting, you will hear a call to reengage in the self-discovery process that can help you get back on track and discover the leader in you. From working with many leaders from all walks of society, we know that when you are in touch with your own vision, values, perspectives, and roles, you will find a rewarding leadership path.

Who are you? Who do you want to be? Where does leadership fit in your life? How would you like the story of your life to be written and its impact measured? If you carefully consider these questions, you will discover the leader in you. With the help of peers, mentors, coaches, and honest feedback, you can develop your leadership capacity with focus, guidance, and encouragement. Stay conscious of where you want to go. Keep moving, keep acting, and keep making conscious choices about where, when, how, and why you lead. And don't forget to enjoy your journey.

REFERENCES

Baker, D., Greenberg, C., & Yalof, I. (2008). *What happy women know*. New York: Rodale.

Boushey, H., & O'Leary, A. (Eds.). (2009). *The Shriver report: A woman's nation changes everything*. Washington, DC: Center for American Progress. Retrieved from http://www.americanprogress.org/issues/2009/10/pdf/awn/a_womans _nation.pdf

Buckingham, M., & Clifton, D. O. (2001). *Now discover your strengths*. New York: Free Press.

Calarco, A., & Gurvis, J. (2006). *Adaptability: Responding effectively to change*. Greensboro, NC: Center for Creative Leadership.

Canton, J. (2006). *The extreme future: The top trends that will reshape the world for the next 5, 10, and 20 years*. New York: Dutton.

Cohen, B., & Greenfield, J. (1997). *Ben & Jerry's double-dip: How to run a values-led business and make money, too*. New York: Simon & Schuster.

Collins, G. (2009). *When everything changed: The amazing journey of American women from 1960 to the present*. New York: Little, Brown.

Collins, J. C. (2001). *Good to great: Why some companies make the leap—and others don't*. New York: HarperBusiness.

Criswell, C., & Campbell, D. (2008). *Building an authentic leadership image*. Greensboro, NC: Center for Creative Leadership.

Csikszentmihalyi, M. (1990). *Flow: The psychology of optimal experience*. New York: HarperCollins.

Dalton, M. A. (1998). *Becoming a more versatile learner*. Greensboro, NC: Center for Creative Leadership.

Deal, J. (2007). *Retiring the generation gap: How employees young and old can find common ground*. San Francisco: Jossey-Bass.

Desvaux, G., Devillard-Hoellinger, S., & Meaney, M. C. (2008). A business case for women. *McKinsey Quarterly*, *4*, 26–33.

Drath, W. H., & Palus, C. J. (1994). *Making common sense: Leadership as meaning-making in a community of practice*. Greensboro, NC: Center for Creative Leadership.

Drucker, P. F. (1995). *Managing in a time of great change*. New York: Truman Talley/Dutton.

Drucker, P. F. (2001). *The essential Drucker*. New York: HarperCollins.

Dweck, C. S. (2006). *Mindset: The new psychology of success*. New York: Random House.

Ernst, C., & Yip, J. (2008). Bridging boundaries: Meeting the challenge of workplace diversity. *Leadership in Action*, *28*(1), 3–6.

Fiorina, C. (2006). *Tough choices: A memoir*. New York: Penguin.

Florida, R. (2005, October). The world in numbers: The world is spiky. *Atlantic Monthly*, 48–51. Retrieved from http://www.creativeclass.com/rfcgdb/articles/other-2005-The%20World%20is%20Spiky.pdf

Frankl, V. E. (1959). *Man's search for meaning*. Boston: Beacon Press.

Friedman, T. L. (2005). *The world is flat: A brief history of the twenty-first century*. New York: Farrar, Straus and Giroux.

Gentry, W. A., & Chappelow, C. T. (2009). Managerial derailment: Weaknesses that can be fixed. In R. B. Kaiser (Ed.), *The perils of accentuating the positive* (pp. 97–113). Tulsa, OK: Hogan Press.

Grayson, C., & Baldwin, D. (2007). *Leadership networking: Connect, collaborate, create*. Greensboro, NC: Center for Creative Leadership, 2007.

Greenleaf, R. K. (1991). *Servant leadership: A journey into the nature of legitimate power and greatness*. New York: Paulist Press.

Hall, D. T., Hannum, K. M., & McCarthy, J. F. (2009). Leadership experience: What is it and what counts? *Leadership in Action, 29*(1), 21–22.

Hammonds, K. H. (2004). Balance is bunk! *Fast Company, 87*, 68–76.

Hannum, K. M. (2007). *Social identity: Knowing yourself, leading others*. Greensboro, NC: Center for Creative Leadership.

Hannum, K. M., & Hoole, E. (2009). *Tracking your development*. Greensboro, NC: Center for Creative Leadership.

Harburg, E. Y., & Saidy, F. (Book); Harburg, E. Y. (Lyrics); Lane, B. (Music). (1947). *Finian's Rainbow*.

Hedberg, M. (2003). Movie plot. *On Mitch all together* [CD]. New York: Comedy Central Records.

Heifetz, R. A., & Linsky, M. (2002). *Leadership on the line: Staying alive through the dangers of leading*. Boston: Harvard Business School Press.

Kaplan, R. E. *Skillscope*. (1997). Greensboro, NC: Center for Creative Leadership.

Kaplan, R. E., Drath, W. H., and Kofodimos, J. R. (1991). *Beyond ambition: How driven managers can lead better and live better*. San Francisco: Jossey-Bass.

Kossek, E. E., & Lautsch, B. A. (2008). *CEO of me: Creating a life that works in the flexible job age*. Upper Saddle River, NJ: Wharton School Publishing.

Kundera, M. (1984). *The unbearable lightness of being*. New York: HarperCollins.

Lencioni, P. (2008). *The three big questions for a frantic family: A leadership fable about restoring sanity to the most important organization in your life*. San Francisco: Jossey-Bass.

Lombardo, M. M., & McCauley, C. D. *Benchmarks*. (2000). Greensboro, NC: Center for Creative Leadership.

Lyness, K. S., & Judiesch, M. K. (2008). Can a manager have a life and a career? International and multisource perspectives on work-life balance and career advancement potential. *Journal of Applied Psychology, 93*, 789–805.

McAdams, D. P. (2006). *The person: A new introduction to personality psychology*. Hoboken, NJ: Wiley.

McCauley, C. D. (2006). *Developmental assignments: Creating learning experiences without changing jobs*. Greensboro, NC: Center for Creative Leadership.

McCauley, C. D., & Douglas, C. A. (2004). Developmental relationships. In C. D. McCauley & E. Van Velsor (Eds.), *The Center for Creative leadership handbook of leadership development* (2nd ed.). San Francisco: Jossey-Bass.

McDowell-Larsen, S. (2009, August 12). Sweating it: Why leaders need to exercise. *Washington Post*. Retrieved March 9, 2010, from http://views.washingtonpost.com/leadership/guestinsights/2009/08/sweating-it-why-leaders-need-to-exercise.html

McGuire, J. B., & Rhodes, G. B. (2009). *Transforming your leadership culture*. San Francisco: Jossey-Bass.

Musselwhite, C., & Jones, R. (2004). *Dangerous opportunity: Making change work*. Bloomington, IN: Xlibris.

Pearce, T. (1995). *Leading out loud: The authentic speaker, the credible leader*. San Francisco: Jossey-Bass.

Pearce, T. (2003). *Leading out loud: Inspiring change through authentic communication* (New and rev. ed.). San Francisco: Jossey-Bass.

Peters, T. (2001, February 28). Rule #3: Leadership is confusing as hell. *Fast Company, 44*. Retrieved from http://www.fastcompany.com/magazine/44/rules.html?page=0%2C4

Reeve, C. (1999). *Still me*. New York: Ballantine Books.

Rock, D. (2009). *Brain at work: Strategies for overcoming distraction, regaining focus, and working smarter all day long*. New York: HarperCollins.

Rowling, J. K. (1998). *Harry Potter and the sorcerer's stone*. New York: Scholastic Press.

Ruderman, M., Graves, L., & Ohlott, P. (2007). Managers can benefit from personal lives. *Leadership in Action, 26*(6), 8–11.

Ruderman, M. N., Ohlott, P. J., Panzer, K., & King, S. N. (1999). How managers view success. *Leadership in Action, 18*(6), 6–10.

Ruderman, M. N., Ohlott, P. J., Panzer, K., & King, S. N. (2002). Benefits of multiple roles for managerial women. *Academy of Management Journal, 45*(2), 369–386.

Sacks, O. (1970). *The man who mistook his wife for a hat*. New York: Simon & Schuster.

Schwartz, T. (2007). Manage your energy, not your time. *Harvard Business Review, 85*(10), 63–73.

Shapiro, D. J., Jr. (1978). *Precision Nirvana*. Upper Saddle River, NJ: Prentice Hall.

Shipman, C., & Kay, K. (2009). *Womenomics: Write your own rules for success: How to stop juggling and struggling and finally start living and working the way you really want*. New York: HarperCollins.

Silverstein, M. J., & Sayre, K. (2009). The female economy. *Harvard Business Review, 87*(9), 46–53.

Tuna, C., & Lublin, J. S. (2009, July 14). Welch: "No such thing as work-life balance." *Wall Street Journal*. Retrieved from http://online.wsj.com/article/SB124726415198325373.html

Tye, J. (2008). *The twelve core action values: Workbook for the values coach guided self-coaching course*. Solon, IA: Values Coach.

Vaill, P. B. (1989). *Managing as a performing art: New ideas for a world of chaotic change*. San Francisco: Jossey-Bass.

Wilhelm, W. (1996). Learning from past leaders. In F. Hesselbein, M. Goldsmith, & R. Beckhard (Eds.), *The leader of the future: New visions, strategies, and practices for the next era* (pp. 221–226). San Francisco: Jossey-Bass.

Winter, A. (2009, November 29). Survey: Most employees prefer current position over boss's. *Greensboro News and Record*, p. F1.

Wood, J. (2006). *Leaving Microsoft to change the world: An entrepreneur's odyssey to educate the world's children*. New York: HarperCollins.

"You've got to find what you love," Jobs says. (2005, June 14). *Stanford Report*. Retrieved from http://news.stanford.edu/news/2005/june15/jobs-061505.html

ABOUT THE AUTHORS

SARA N. KING, principal of Optimum Insights, Inc., helps leaders explore their potential and increase their performance through her expertise as an executive coach, keynote speaker, author, workshop designer, and facilitator. During twenty-five years in leadership development, she has served thousands of executives in Fortune 500 companies, government agencies, educational institutions, and nonprofits. Throughout two decades at the Center for Creative Leadership, Sara held roles as a global executive, trainer, program manager, and researcher. She began her extensive work in the field of women's leadership in 1986 as a member of the Breaking the Glass Ceiling research team, which studied the career development of executive women in Fortune 100 firms. That team produced the 1987 book *Breaking the Glass Ceiling: Can Women Reach the Top of America's Largest Corporations?* by Ann Morrison, Randall White, and Ellen Van Velsor. Sara's passion for women's leadership includes her eighteen-year relationship with the national Women in Cable Telecommunications organization, where she is a facilitator in the flagship leadership program. Sara earned her B.A. in English from Wake Forest University and an M.S. in higher education administration from Cornell University. She serves on the advisory board for the University of North Carolina-Greensboro undergraduate school of business and the advisory board of Discovery Learning. She can be contacted at saraking@optimuminsights.com.

—

DAVID G. ALTMAN is executive vice president of research, innovation, and product development at the Center for Creative Leadership. Previously he spent ten years as professor and associate professor of public health sciences and of pediatrics at the Wake Forest University School of Medicine in Winston-Salem, North Carolina, and ten years as a senior research scientist (and postdoctoral fellow and research associate) at Stanford University School of Medicine in Palo Alto, California. He has published over one hundred journal articles, book chapters, and books. He received his M.A. and Ph.D. degrees in social ecology from the University of California, Irvine, and his B.A. in psychology from the University of California, Santa Barbara. He has served as national program director of the Robert Wood Johnson Foundation (RWJF) Substance Abuse Policy Research Program, a $66 million, investigator-initiated research initiative. He has also served as conational program director of the RWJF Ladder to Leadership Program, a $4 million leadership development program for nonprofit leaders in health and health care and as conational program director of the RWJF Executive Nurse Fellows Program. In 1997, he was selected as one of forty Americans to participate in the three-year W. K. Kellogg Foundation National Leadership Program. David is a fellow of three divisions of the American Psychological Association and the Society of Behavioral Medicine. He is also a member of the American Public Health Association, Council on Epidemiology and Prevention of the American Heart Association, the Society of Public Health Education, and Academy of Behavioral Medicine Research. He can be contacted at altmand@ccl.org.

—

ROBERT J. LEE is a management consultant and executive coach in private practice in New York City. He is the director of iCoach-NewYork, which provides coach training programs and supervision for internal and external coaches. He is on the adjunct faculty at the Milano Graduate School of New School University and is a senior fellow with the Zicklin School of Business, Baruch College, City University of New York. From 1994 to 1997, he was president and CEO of the Center for Creative Leadership. Prior to his service at CCL, Bob was founder and president of Lee Hecht Harrison, a worldwide career services firm. He is a coauthor of *Executive Coaching: A Guide for the HR Professional* (Jossey-Bass/Pfeiffer, 2005). He is a fellow of the Society for Industrial and Organizational Psychology and a member of the Society of Consulting Psychology and the Society of Psychologists in Management (SPIM). He received the Distinguished Psychologist in Management award in 2008 from SPIM. His Ph.D. is in industrial/organizational psychology from Case Western Reserve University. He may be reached at bob@bobleecoach.com.

INDEX

Pearce, T., 84, 89

Personal life: drift and, 8–9; as element of Discovering Leadership Framework, xii, 11, 13; experiences in, 99, 116; impact of, on work, 123–125; impact of work on, 122–123; opportunities for leadership in, 17–18; transfer of work lessons to, 130–132. *See also* Work-life balance

Personal values. *See* Core values

Personal vision, leadership vision and, 50–53

Peters, T., 84

Power, 61, 62–63

Pragmatists, 110–111

Purpose. *See* Leadership purpose

Q

Questions for reflection: on change styles, 111; on changes in organizational realities, 25, 26, 31, 33, 34, 36–37; on context for leadership, 48; on drift, 9; on improving work-life balance, 141, 142, 143–145; on leadership competencies, 105–106; on leadership motivation, 94; on leadership profile, 119; on leadership roles, 107; on leadership values, 94; on leadership vision, 56, 58, 59–60, 61, 62–63, 64, 65, 66, 67–68; on learning from experiences, 113, 114–115; on learning styles, 109; on relationship between work and

personal life, 123, 125; on view of leadership, 42; on work-life balance, 133–134, 136, 146

R

Recession of 2008, 32

Reeve, C., 57–58

Relationships, developmental, 164–167

Resources, work-life balance and, 139, 145

Rewards: of leadership, 47, 136–138; as leadership motivation, 71–72

Rhodes, G. B., 35

Richardson, H. S., 84

Risk taking, 85–88

Rock, D., 130

Role models, 60–61. *See also* Heroes

Rowling, J. K., 57

Ruderman, M. N., 129, 131

S

Sacks, O., 55

Saidy, F., 58

Sayre, K., 29

Schwartz, T., 130, 134

Self-image, 57

Self-knowledge, techniques for obtaining, 99. *See also* Leadership profile

Sequencing, to improve work-life balance, 139, 144–145

Servant leadership, 39, 40–41, 74

Service, as leadership motivation, 74–75

ABOUT THE CENTER FOR CREATIVE LEADERSHIP

The Center for Creative Leadership (CCL) is a top-ranked, global provider of executive education that unlocks individual and organizational potential through its exclusive focus on leadership education and research. Founded in 1970 as a nonprofit educational institution, CCL helps clients worldwide cultivate creative leadership—the capacity to achieve more than imagined by thinking and acting beyond boundaries—through an array of programs, products, and other services.

CCL ranked number 3 overall in the 2010 *Financial Times* worldwide survey of executive education and was ranked in the top 5 by *BusinessWeek* in 2009. It is headquartered in Greensboro, North Carolina, with campuses in Colorado Springs, Colorado; San Diego, California; Brussels, Belgium; and Singapore; and with offices in several cities in India and in Moscow, Russia, and Addis Ababa, Ethiopia. Supported by more than 450 faculty members and staff, it works annually with more than twenty thousand leaders and two thousand organizations. In addition, fourteen Network Associates around the world offer selected CCL programs and assessments.

CCL draws strength from its nonprofit status and educational mission, which provide unusual flexibility in a world where quarterly profits often drive thinking and direction. It has the freedom to be objective, wary of short-term trends, and motivated foremost by its mission—hence, its substantial and sustained investment in leadership research. Although CCL's work is always grounded in a strong foundation of research, it focuses on achieving a beneficial impact in the real world. Its efforts are geared to be practical and action oriented, helping leaders and their organizations more effectively achieve their goals and vision. The desire to transform learning and ideas into action provides the impetus for CCL's programs, assessments, publications, and services.

Capabilities

CCL's activities encompass leadership education, knowledge generation and dissemination, and building a community centered on leadership. CCL is broadly recognized for excellence in executive education, leadership development, and innovation by sources such as *Business Week, Financial Times, Forbes,* the *Washington Post,* the *New York Times,* and the *Wall Street Journal.*

Open-Enrollment Programs

Fifteen open-enrollment courses are designed for leaders at all levels, as well as people responsible for leadership development and training at their organizations. This portfolio offers distinct choices for participants seeking a particular learning environment or type of experience. Some programs are structured specifically around small group activities, discussion, and personal reflection, while others offer hands-on opportunities through business simulations, artistic exploration, team-building exercises, and new-skills practice. Many of these programs offer private one-on-one sessions with a feedback coach.

For a complete listing of open-enrollment programs and the Leader Development Roadmap, visit http://www.ccl.org/leadership/programs/index.aspx.

Customized Programs

CCL develops tailored educational solutions for more than one hundred client organizations around the world each year. Through this applied practice, CCL structures and delivers programs focused on specific leadership development needs within the context of defined organizational challenges, including innovation, the merging of cultures, and the development of a broader pool of leaders. The objective is to help organizations develop, within their own cultures, the leadership capacity they need to address challenges as they emerge.

Program details are available at http://www.ccl.org/leadership/solutions/index.aspx.

Coaching

CCL's suite of coaching services is designed to help leaders maintain a sustained focus and generate increased momentum toward achieving their goals. These coaching alternatives vary in depth and duration and serve a variety of needs, from helping an executive sort through career and life issues to working with an organization to integrate coaching into its internal development process. Our coaching offerings, which can supplement program attendance or be customized for specific individual or team needs, are based on our model of assessment, challenge, and support (ACS).

Learn more about CCL's coaching services at http://www.ccl.org/leadership/coaching/index.aspx.

Assessment and Development Resources

CCL pioneered 360-degree feedback and believes that assessment provides a solid foundation for learning, growth, and transformation and that development truly happens when an individual recognizes the need to change. CCL offers a broad selection of assessment tools, online resources, and simulations that can help individuals, teams, and organizations increase their self-awareness, facilitate their own learning, enable their development, and enhance their effectiveness.

CCL's assessments are profiled at http://www.ccl.org/leadership/assessments/index.aspx.

Publications

The theoretical foundation for many of our programs, as well as the results of CCL's extensive and often groundbreaking research, can be found in the scores of publications issued by CCL Press and through the center's alliance with Jossey-Bass, a Wiley imprint. Among these are landmark works, such as *Breaking the Glass Ceiling* and *The Lessons of Experience,* as well as quick-read guidebooks focused on core aspects of leadership. CCL publications provide insights and practical advice to help individuals become more effective leaders, develop leadership training within organizations, address issues of change and diversity, and build the systems and strategies that advance leadership collectively at the institutional level.

A complete listing of CCL publications is available at http://www.ccl.org/leadership/publications/index.aspx.

Leadership Community

To ensure that its work remains focused, relevant, and important to the individuals and organizations it serves, CCL maintains a host of networks, councils, and learning and virtual communities that bring together alumni, donors, faculty, practicing leaders, and thought leaders from around the globe. CCL also forges relationships and alliances with individuals, organizations, and associations that share its values and mission. The energy, insights, and support from these relationships help shape and sustain CCL's educational and research practices and provide its clients with an added measure of motivation and inspiration as they continue their lifelong commitment to leadership and learning.

To learn more, visit http://www.ccl.org/leadership/community/index.aspx.

Research

CCL's portfolio of programs, products, and services is built on a solid foundation of behavioral science research. The role of research at CCL is to advance the understanding of leadership and transform learning into practical tools for participants and clients. CCL's research is the hub of a cycle that transforms knowledge into applications and applications into knowledge, thereby illuminating the way organizations think about and enact leadership and leader development.

Find out more about current research initiatives at http://www.ccl.org/leadership/research/index.aspx.

For additional information about CCL, visit http://www.ccl.org or call Client Services at 336-545-2810.